W9-CCW-905

1st Printing: 9/94;
2nd, 6/95; 3rd, 10/96;
4th, 9/97; 5th, 4/99;
6th, 1/01; 7th, 6/02;
8th, 3/04; 9th, 6/05;
10th, 12/06; 11th, 10/08;
12th, 7/09; 13th, 6/12;
14th, 3/14 ; 15th, 2/17

Publication #11 in the "On Target"
Series of Outdoor Sports Publications
from Glenn Helgeland's
TARGET COMMUNICATIONS

BECOME THE ARROW

by Byron Ferguson
with Glenn Helgeland

Library of Congress Number: 92-83909

TARGET COMMUNICATIONS CORPORATION
7626 W. Donges Bay Rd.
Mequon, WI 53097

ISBN: 0-913305-09-X

i

DEDICATION

This is dedicated to my Dad and to all Dads who took the time to teach us young whippersnappers about hunting and ethics.

CONTENTS

• The author with a fine Alabama whitetail.

Biographical Sketch: BYRON FERGUSON

Byron Ferguson, a native of northern Alabama, has been hunting as long as he has been old enough to legally do so. He's still at it in a big way. "I hunt *something* at least 150 days a year," he says. Depending upon the time of year, this could be deer or various other big game, small game, turkey, varmints or carp.

When he began, it was with firearms, then recurve bow, then compound bow .... and then, in a supreme leap "backward" in equipment use but forward, definitely forward, in success and satisfaction regarding his archery shooting and bowhunting, he retired everything else and went strictly to modern barebow shooting with the longbow .... the bow of Robin Hood, the bow of Howard Hill. It was and is

●*The mirror shot is one of many in Ferguson's trick shooting demonstrations, above left. Above right, Larry Bauman, left, Byron Ferguson, center, and Glenn Helgeland, on an Ontario hunt. The three took three bears with three arrows. Bauman's bear, shown, scored 20-9/16. Lower left, Ferguson signs an autograph for a fan at the Wisconsin Bowhunters Association fall outdoor shoot.*

fitting, for the late Howard Hill, also an Alabaman, has long been Ferguson's hero. To say that he fell in love with this style of shooting would be an understatement.

Over the years, but almost exclusively since he began barebow shooting with the longbow, Ferguson has tagged more than 100 white-tail deer, a couple of black bears (one of which qualifies for the Pope & Young Club record book), a fine Newfoundland bull moose, and countless small game and upland birds.

Byron, however, is more than a hunter. Much more. Ferguson is an archery demonstration shooter....archery trick shot, if you will.

● Ferguson on an Italian national television program titled "In Search of The Arc". "This show was live, and we were asked to return for an encore. I'd gone through my repertoire, so Wanda and I had to come up with a couple of new shots. We managed it, but there was some cold sweating for a while."

● Chambord Castle in France, site of the game fair where Ferguson performed before 75,000 people. The castle has 365 rooms....a room for every day of the year.

Today, he shoots longbow archery just about 365 days a year....366 days in Leap Year. He gives dozens of performances annually at deer shows, sportsmen's shows, club and association events. In the first half of 1994 alone, his cumulative audiences totaled more than 250,000 people.

He has performed on Japanese national television, Canadian national television, and in France, Italy, Spain and Chile. He was the first American archer to perform in France since the legendary Howard Hill in the 1940s. Ferguson performed before live audiences of 75,000 people at the French Game Fair at Chambord Castle. Ferguson was declared "King of the Fair", an award which is decided by the number of standing ovations the performers receive. He was referred to in the French press as "The White Indian", for he has enough Creek and Cherokee blood in his lineage to qualify for Indian treaty rights hunting if he wanted to, which he doesn't.

The most nerve-wracking shot he has been asked to make was on Japanese national television, where he put an arrow through the finger opening of a diamond ring valued at $17,000. "I was praying the 'you break it; you buy it' principal wasn't in effect right then," he says.

● *Ferguson on Japanese national television. He has just shot an arrow through a well-shaken can of beer, which resulted in a lot of liquid spraying around. His toughest shot ever was on this show — putting an arrow through the finger hole of a $17,000 diamond ring.*

● *Gallon plastic milk jugs, with a loose weight inside for easier and better throwing and flight, make excellent wing-shooting practice. The arrow in flight looks good.*

● *Young Zachary Ferguson, a few years ago, developing his longbow shooting form. Ferguson teaches three-fingers-under to people just learning to shoot barebow. This style makes aiming down the arrow easiest and gets good results right away, which makes the new archer happy and makes the coach think he's smart.*

● *The growing interest in traditional archery produces a group of archers after every demonstration, eager to get questions answered and learn more. This session was at the Wisconsin Bowhunters Association fall outdoor shoot.*

At the moment, Byron is working hard developing his own television program for cable outlets. It will be known as "The World of Adventure."

Ferguson also is a longbow manufacturer. His handcrafted traditional longbows are produced and sold worldwide through Ferguson Adventure Archery.

He is sought out by celebrities from motion pictures, television, the recording industry and the professional sports world to teach them his style of bow and arrow shooting. He has worked with such people as Don Johnson, Dickey Betts, Gary Morris, Marshall Teague, Will Clark and Steve Kanaly.

Byron is an honorary member of the Federation des Chasseurs a l'Arc; national bowhunting organizations in Germany and Italy; in 1993 was made an Honorary Leftenant in the Canadian Rangers (Newfoundland), which is similar to a National Guard, specializing in search and rescue; lifetime member of the National Rifle Association; member of the Alabama Society of Traditional Bowmen.

Byron Ferguson is a man dedicated to attaining the highest levels of performance in bowhunting and the production of superior equipment for the sport. He is also a committed conservationist who strives to teach outdoor ethics and sportsmanship to all those he touches. For the last four years, the Ferguson Archery Tournament, sponsored by the Alabama Society of Traditional Bowmen, has attracted hundreds of archers from across the nation and raised thousands of dollars for Alabama's Children's Hospital.

Byron Ferguson, his wife Wanda, and their sons Shaun and Zachary, live near Hartselle, Alabama.

● News media respond well to photogenic, colorful action. Traditional archery isn't mainstream society, but it speaks of Robin Hood and romance and simpler times. Put a name, a spokesperson, out there for the media....and the result is more exposure for the sport of archery.

● Every good shooting act demands teamwork. The person throwing the targets is just as important as the shooter, if not more important, for the targets must be tossed consistently time after time after time. Wanda Ferguson handles that important part of the archery trick shooting demonstrations with grace and aplomb. It appears here that she had her hands full with a question on the Japanese television program, and Byron wasn't quite sure how she was going to answer it.

Chapter 1
Becoming The Arrow

What is "Become The Arrow"?

What is "become the arrow?" It's a philosophy, a belief, a projection of self and of self-confidence, a tremendous amount of concentration. No it isn't Zen, but it certainly is much more than mechanical and/or technical success. It's a way of knowing and believing in your archery gear and in yourself that heightens your enjoyment of shooting and ought to heighten your success.

For anyone wanting to learn barebow shooting, **"become the arrow" is the most efficient, easiest to learn, most forgiving and easiest barebow shooting style to repeat, shot after shot, under stress conditions.** That's a strong statement, but I stand wholeheartedly behind it. In the development of the philosophy and technique of "become the arrow", I tried every type of barebow shooting.

In bowhunting, "become the arrow" has more to do with a state of mind, an attitude, a commitment.....a preparedness. A couple of springs ago, I was in a bear hunting camp with half a dozen other guys. Three of us shot traditional gear and spent a lot of time outside the cabins with our bows, shooting at informal targets but essentially playing with bows and arrows, keeping sharp, enjoying the activity. We invited a couple of other guys to shoot with us, but they declined because, as they explained, "We've already got our sights set". We weren't talking about figuring out where to aim at various distances; we were talking about just enjoying archery.

I don't know if there was any relationship, but they wounded and lost three bears, with no shot longer than 15 yards.

It's understandable, then, that the path to becoming a competent barebow shooter is hard work. However, hard work alone won't do it. It has to be properly set up and properly directed, because there's a considerable difference between working hard and working smart. You can work hard but not smart; all you do is spin your wheels and not get the job done. You can work smart but not hard; all you do is get a good start but never reach the goal. Obviously, a combination of the two is the best.

A few years ago, I talked to a mountain man type of gentleman who said he never read anything because he was too busy living. On the surface that sounds pretty good, but let's take another look. He's struggling along, making traditional equipment of all sorts, sort of a throwback to the mountain men in clothing and gear, and maybe even further back, to the Indians, in archery gear.

But without research, without checking the mistakes others have made, without determining what others have learned before him, he's reinventing the wheel. He's also taking a long time to get somewhere.

Is he having fun? Apparently. Is he satisfied? Apparently. Is he working hard? Definitely. Is he working smart? I don't think so.

That's why I say "Let's look at where we've been, to see where we must go in becoming the arrow." Archery coaches have taught us for years to become the bow. They say, "Make the bow an extension of yourself." To me, that seems short-sighted and misdirected. The bow does not take any animals unless you use it as a club and beat them with it. The bow doesn't score any points in an archery contest unless you use it as a spear and throw it into the bullseye, for which you probably would be disqualified. Therefore, **if you're going to make part of your equipment an extension of yourself, make the arrow that extension. It's what counts.**

I suppose, if you wanted to carry the point further, you could say the target point or field point scores points, and the broadhead takes game. However, that arrow tip is just that...only the tip, part of the whole. The entire arrow -- nock, fletching, shaft and tip -- working together properly produce the desired result.

James Dickey, author of the book "Deliverance", said in an interview published in *Archery World* magazine in the early 1970s, "You see the flight of the arrow, which for me is the prettiest thing in sports. There's nothing to compare with the sail of a really nice 60-65 yard shot. The arc of the arrow at that range is almost unbearably beautiful. It gives the illusion of predestination...it seems to be following a string right to the place you want it to go. That's *you* going out there, *you* making that flight."

He added, "There's a marvelous complexity to archery...with the mechanics of a bow, an arrow, a string...with the physical complexity of your bow hand and arm, your drawing hand, anchor and release. But if you can keep it simple in your own mind, don't let the elements run away with you, it all ends with a surpassingly beautiful simplicity -- the simple shooting of an arrow."

If you want to be an average archer, just practice. If you want to become a good archer, practice until the bow becomes an extension of you. If you want to become better than good, practice until the arrow becomes an extension of yourself. Practice smart. Always practice smart. No excuses. Honest with yourself. Anything else is wheel spinning.

What does the achieved mental extension accomplish? It puts the concentration down-range on the target, where it belongs, rather than at arm's length, as if you were using sights. When you reach the goal, the bow disappears, becomes non-existent.

The bow is not as important as the arrow; that's what it boils down to. If you think the bow is so important, go out in your back yard and cut a slender sapling. Make it into an arrow. Buy a $1,000 custom bow and see how well you can shoot that green stick arrow. On the other hand, spend $40 on a set of decent arrows, go out to your back yard and find a sapling big enough to make into a bow. Those arrows will shoot consistently. That's why I say the arrow is much more important than the bow.

The Japanese, the experts of zen, say to become the target. If you become so consumed in your concentration that there is nothing in the world remaining but the target, the whole world becomes the target. How can you possibly miss? That's how I understand the definition of zen as it applies to archery. I know this is an extremely simplified definition, but I also can't see any sense in tying us all in mental knots trying to go any deeper, especially since I don't agree with it.

I believe our western world sports philosophy is more applicable. If you go into any game or activity with the attitude "I'm not going to lose," or you spend your mental preparation time telling yourself "Don't lose", you're probably going to lose. If you try not to lose, you're probably going to lose because you're not playing to win. You need to play to win.

The same attitude, slightly modified, applies to shooting archery. It's just another way of developing a strong positive attitude and working to make something good happen, as long as the emphasis remains on the development of self and of your skills. **Archery is a**

● *Archery is a sport where control of the self is paramount; much of the effort and development is internalized. You have to build on strengths but practice your weak points. You cannot go into the hunt or the field range or the exhibition stage thinking "just don't miss", because that's negative. The only pressure that exists, you put on yourself.*

sport where control of the self is paramount; much of the effort and development is internalized.

If you go into the hunt with the thought of "Just don't miss", you're either going to miss or you won't even shoot because you're afraid you'll miss. You have to go in there with the attitude that "I am going to take the shot, and I'm going to put the arrow exactly right there." And know that you can do it.

Concentration, full concentration, must be on the making of each shot. Let me try to describe the progressive mental picture of concentration.

Most beginning archers, when they are still more concerned about keeping the arrow on the arrow rest than most other things, see the target as part of a large picture, the target and all the surroundings. As they become more adept, they don't have to worry about such mechanical things as keeping the arrow on the arrow rest or the nock on the string. Then their sight picture of the target begins to shrink to where they see the target and only a few feet on either side of the target. They become better shots. The next step up in the progression of concentration is to see basically just the target....still a little fuzz around the edges, but the edges are out of focus. The target is in full focus.

You reach a point where your concentration level is so high that it is almost like having tunnel vision. You're still vaguely aware of what's happening around you, but the spot you want to hit comes into sharp focus while everything else is blurred, even the other parts of the target. If, during an exhibition, I hear the crowd noises behind me, or even so much as sense the audience behind me, then most likely its not going to be a good shot. I'm allowing too much outside interference; my concentration level isn't high enough.

Before you let the arrow go on a perfect shot, you know it will be a perfect shot. Your concentration level is so high, everything is in perfect focus. When you see it that way, that is the key. If, when you get ready to shoot, the target is a little bit out of focus, the shot is probably going to be a pretty good shot, but it won't be a perfect shot. **With the perfect shot, there is a sense of perfection before the bowstring ever slips free**, because the visual picture in your brain is the ideal one, the correct one. The clear picture your eyes see gives a clear message to the brain, and it says, "This is going to be good, guys. I feel goooood. It's gonna work."

To make this work, you have to be able to focus on the target, concentrate on the target....and then stay there. You can't shift from target to reference to target. This level of concentration is not something which can be done on command. I still must work at it on a daily basis.

I need to modify that a bit. When you're beginning to learn "become the arrow", you have to split your concentration between the target and the arrow tip reference point in order to in-grain into your subconscious what the sight picture looks like for a good shot. As you progress, your concentration will be more applied to the target than anything else, and you will eventually get to the point where if anyone were to ask you "How do you aim?", the response would be "I just look at what I want to hit."

Interestingly enough, age has something to do with it. The older you become, the more patient you become. The more patient you are, the better you'll work at developing the concentration and skill levels necessary to succeed.

Let me give you an example of what happened last year at one of my exhibitions. I was doing a show in Myrtle Beach, South Carolina. When I walked into the auditorium that day and looked at my target butt, the center of the bullseye of that target butt just jumped out. It was in such perfect focus that I knew we were going to have a good show that day.

As I was warming up, I shot three arrows into the center of the bullseye. I noticed a small boy in the front row close to me, and I told him "See that third arrow I just shot into the bullseye? Keep your eye

● *If your concentration is not fully on the shot, then the information given to your mental computer will be erroneous or incomplete. But with "become the arrow", when your concentration is right, the target is in wonderfully clear focus and you have the feeling you can't miss. "The best for me was the time I Robin Hooded a shot during a trick shooting performance. It's great to have witnesses when things go right."*

on it."

When I turned back to face the target, the nock of that arrow was in such perfect focus it was almost like I was looking through a rifle scope. I drew and shot and sure enough Robin-Hooded that arrow.

What "become the arrow" accomplishes is simple -- it focuses the information we are giving to our brain, to our mental computer, into a narrow band. By doing this it eliminates the unnecessary and distracting "noise" that would be coming in from our other senses. What we are interested in here is the ability of the brain to take the information given it, and then make the necessary computations to allow us to make an accurate shot.

If you are distracted, if your concentration is not fully on the shot, then the information given to your mental computer would be erroneous. Like any computer, if you give it the wrong information the outcome of the computation is going to be wrong. GIGO, in computer slang, means Garbage In/Garbage Out. In archery, that means a bad shot.

The feeling I had with that Robin-Hooded arrow was like I had just downed a bull elk, a new world record elk. It was a rush. I knew before I ever fired the arrow, before I ever drew the bow, that I could do that shot. I knew I could make it. I've had days when I felt like I didn't know for sure whether that I was going to hit the target butt. But on that particular day it was quite an achievement, quite a feeling. I'd like to be able to do that all the time. I'd like to say that I can do that all the time, but I'd be lying. That is, however, always what we're striving for. That's what becoming the arrow is all about....to strive to become the arrow on every shot, knowing full well going into it that we're not going to be able to do it on every shot.

WHY SHOOT BAREBOW?

It's pretty doggone obvious that anyone with modern compound bows, with a minimal amount of practice, can go out on the target range at long distances and shoot rings around me or anyone else shooting traditional equipment. We cannot shoot as consistently accurate as they can with that equipment.

It's also true that no one can take a .30/30 lever action rifle and expect to compete against a person using a bench rest rifle. However, how many people do you know who hunt with a benchrest rifle? With the more modern equipment, add-on accessories become more important and are more available. The more-modern basic equipment makes it easier to shoot more accurately with less practice, and the accessories just add to that condition. However, with the sight, you have to know the distance, pick the pin, get the pin on the target, solidify the aim, and then shoot. That takes time, more time than may be available.

There are those of us who still prefer the old single shot rifles or the lever action rifles and longbows or barebow recurves for our hunting. To us they make more sense and are more fun. No one NEEDS all that other stuff. You don't need the scope on the bow. You don't need the mechanical release. You don't need the stabilizer. Sure, they may be nice, but you don't need all the other gadgets to shoot an animal that on the national average is going to be standing 18 to 23 steps from you.

For most of us shooting traditional archery equipment, or any archery equipment, it is just more fun to shoot barebow style. Traditional equipment -- in attitude, in philosophy, in *tradition* -- cries out to be shot barebow. It was not intended to have mechanical things taped, screwed or glued onto it.

It requires more involvement -- the commitment I spoke of earlier -- to get the ultimate in enjoyment for this style of archery and bowhunting. But I also believe that the more you put into it, the more you get back out of it. You're more than just a technically competent

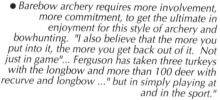

● *Barebow archery requires more involvement, more commitment, to get the ultimate in enjoyment for this style of archery and bowhunting. "I also believe that the more you put into it, the more you get back out of it. Not just in game"... Ferguson has taken three turkeys with the longbow and more than 100 deer with recurve and longbow ..." but in simply playing at and in the sport."*

shooter going out and sitting on a treestand. It's like so much specialization -- the more you know, the more you realize there is to know, and the more joy you get out of it. I agree, there sometimes is some narrow-mindedness among traditional archers, but there's no superficiality to the practice and enjoyment of traditional archery. If you're going to be competent at it and enjoy it, it forces you to leap in with both feet. That's the old "ham and eggs" syndrome. The chicken makes a contribution, but the hog makes a total commitment.

I guess we're just hogs for the sport of shooting traditional archery equipment barebow style.

I'm fully aware that if you want to return to the "good old days", just turn off the air conditioning. I'm also aware that barebow

Becoming The Arrow

bowhunting is work when your life depends on it but a joyful challenge when you know there's a dinner available in the freezer.

However....

Talk to a bowhunter who began with traditional gear, either longbow or recurve, switched to a compound, and then switched back to traditional gear. The first response is "Gee, I forgot how light this was to carry. It's kinda nice, not lugging all that hardware through the woods. And when I shoot it, it just goes tunk." Then his eyes light and he grins.

Barebow style has simplicity. It has setup and tuning ease. The gear is light to carry and quiet to shoot. Fewer things can go wrong with it mechanically, which means fewer things to worry about. Barebow is more reliable when hunting because it is less affected by weather and light conditions than is pin shooting.

When you need aiming speed, you can't beat barebow. A running shot is no big thing when you're shooting barebow. If you will trust your mental computer and visualize right, you'll get the range right and get the shot off quickly.

But it is more than all this talk of form and function. Any hunting is an attempt to return, to whatever degree, to a more straightforward time. Using traditional equipment and shooting barebow style is further effort to strip away the layers of mechanical and technical veneer...."Can I do it the way they did it?" The elemental challenge of putting food on the table with those deceivingly simple tools cannot be denied. You succeed or you starve.

It is an intensely personal decision, this freedom to attempt something so basic in one's preferred way. Especially when you accept that the very freedom of the elemental effort and the "stripped down" gear, by that same nature, carries its own constraints. The subtleties, the nuances, lie in the mastering of that traditional gear and in the awareness and understanding of game animal habits and habitat.

It's also, I guess you would say, more gratifying to make a good barebow shot, because you know then that you did it. It wasn't the pin or the scope or whatever type of sighting system you were using on the equipment. It wasn't the release you were using. It wasn't the stabilizer on the bow. What made that shot was YOU through your hours and hours of barebow practice. You were building a belief in yourself, a reliance on your inner being as well as your physical abilities, to make that shot.

A few seasons ago at an Alabama deer camp, a guy drove in late one afternoon for a visit with the camp host. When he saw us out on the lawn shooting our traditional gear he decided to stay longer.

● *Sometimes the arrow channel is limited, but when you learn to visualize the arrow's flight path, you'll train yourself to pick out that path AND notice whether there will be weeds, twigs, leaves or other easily-missed obstructions in that path. You'll also be able to shoot well under low light conditions.*

"I brought my bow, so as long as you're hunting, I guess I'll stay and hunt tonight," he said.

The gentleman proceeded to tear us apart on the practice range with his compound bow and multi-pin sight and other attachments. He was good. But that afternoon he missed eleven good shots at deer. Maybe all his sight pins worked loose between the practice range and his treestand.

At least he launched arrows. Read on....

A couple of years ago, I had a guy hunting who was using a sight and a mechanical release. He came in one evening and told me about a nice six-point buck he had seen that afternoon. The buck was standing only 15 steps from him, but it was too dark to shoot.

I couldn't understand that for a while, because if it was light enough for him to count the points, why couldn't it be light enough to shoot?

He explained that it was so dark he couldn't think which pin he wanted to use without turning the sight light on. And when he did guts it and turn on the sight light, it was just dark enough that the light obscured the deer. He could see the light but not the deer.

In addition, he also couldn't stand up to take the shot. That was because his release was attached to his wrist, and he already had attached his release to the bowstring, so in effect he was attached to the bow with both hands. Yet he needed one hand free to brace against the tree to enable him to stand up.

I do believe I'd have gotten an arrow into the air, with plenty of light to aim accurately.

● *"I believe the longbow has a spirit. Much of it was, at one time, a tree standing in the forest, and any time I go back to the forest with the longbow in hand, I'm actually taking it home again."*

WHY I SHOOT THE LONGBOW

In the spring of 1992, I went to Farmington, New Mexico, to perform at the Civic Center there, at the request of the Four Corners Bowhunters Association. In my audience, since the site was in close proximity to the Navajo reservation, were several Navajos. In fact, I think the audience was mostly Navajo.

At the end of each session, we would have a 30 minute question and answer session. One of the questions I was most often asked was "Why do you shoot the longbow, rather than the recurve or compound?"

My response took in all the usual reasons -- I enjoy it more, I'm accurate with it, it has tradition and the romance of history and tradition, etc.

Then I added that another reason I shoot the longbow is because the longbow has a spirit. A longbow was at one time a tree standing in the forest, and any time I go back to the forest with the longbow in hand, I'm actually taking it home again.

The questioners' response was a lot of head nodding and applause. No statements of response were needed. They knew what I was talking about. They ended up inviting me to the reservation the next day, where we had an archery shooting session with several of the boys. And then I was invited to come back and hunt mule deer with them, at a substantial discount from the standard fee.

Becoming The Arrow   11

Of course, it works both ways. Dickey Betts has a good friend who is a Navajo shaman, a spiritual leader with medicine man overtones. Stewart, the shaman, and Dickey were talking one time about bowhunting, and Stewart said to Dickey, "I used to bowhunt."

Stewart went on, telling Dickey how they had to fast for so many days, then go into the sweat lodge for so many days or hours, and how they had to be dressed by the medicine man before they were properly set up to go hunting.

Dickey took all this in, sort of dumbfounded -- and mightily impressed -- over the elaborateness, the care and attention to detail. Until Stewart said, "Yeah, it got to be so much trouble I just quit hunting."

Chapter 2
The "Become The Arrow" System

BAREBOW SHOOTING

Barebow shooting is just what it sounds like. It is shooting the bow and arrow without a sighting device on the bow. If you attach a sight to your bow then you are no longer shooting barebow.

The difference between shooting barebow and shooting instinctively? Barebow shooters have a number of reference points -- the arrow, the bow hand, the bow, the bowstring. Instinctive shooting is "poking and hoping", where you simply look at the spot you want to hit, draw the bow back and let the arrow fly, hoping it hits the spot you want it to hit. Theoretically, there are no reference points -- neither the arrow, the bow, nor anything else. Howard Hill said he had seen hundreds of instinctive shooters but had never seen a good one.

Of course, the most common -- and accurate -- statement regarding instinctive shooting is that the only time anyone can take a truly instinctive shot is the first shot they ever take. After that, something learned is applied to the aiming decision with every shot. We cannot do anything without learning something from it. Instinct supposedly doesn't require thought or training. However, to improve, we all apply thought and training. We practice.

The type of shooting called instinctive probably ought to be called snap shooting. You see the target and bing, bing; it happens just that quick. But there is conscious learning involved, if not in the actual shot, at least in the training. Otherwise, if you were a poor shot to begin with, you would remain a poor shot, and the only way you could be a good shot would be to have been born that way.

Some of the systems available to the barebow shooter include string walking, face walking, gap shooting (which is closely akin to Howard Hill's split vision method of aiming, if not the same thing), and point-of-aim. Gap shooting and point-of-aim frequently are confused with one another. The basic distinction is that with gap shooting you focus on the target; with point-of-aim, there also is a gap, but it is much larger.

String walking, face walking and point of aim demand that you know the distance to the target. With point of aim, you guess the distance between the target and the tip of the arrow in feet, rather than in inches (as in gap shooting). You don't even look at the target, but at references on the ground between you and the target. It isn't much fun and obviously is totally impractical for hunting. String walking is too cumbersome for hunting and illegal in most tournaments.

Face walking....if I had to do something other than what I'm doing now, face walking would be it. It is faster than other systems. It is somewhat the reverse of gap shooting, in that you raise or lower the anchor to adjust for shot distance, instead of raising or lowering your bow arm as in gap shooting. The closer the target, the higher on the face you anchor. It is just like adjusting the elevation of the rear sight on a rifle.

This book's subtitle says "the art of MODERN barebow shooting". That's what you're going to learn next, along with an explanation of how and why it developed, why it is the modern method and how it differs from the older shooting method developed and made famous by Howard Hill.

There's been considerable misunderstanding of Howard Hill's shooting method. I have heard it said many times that Howard Hill was the greatest instinctive shot who ever lived. Howard Hill was not an instinctive shot. Howard Hill was a gap shooter. He called it the split vision method of aiming. It's nothing more than being able to keep the eyes focused on the spot to be hit, while at the same time being aware of where the arrow tip is positioned in relation to that spot. I use essentially the same thing, updated to take advantage of modern technology and materials not available to Mr. Hill. With a couple of new wrinkles added.

HOW TO MAKE A MODERN BAREBOW SHOT

Much has been written and discussed about "proper" shooting form. Archery form, as far as I'm concerned, is putting the doggone arrow in the bullseye, no matter how it happens to get there. That is ultimately what we are searching for. There is more to it than that, of course, because we've got to be consistent. For most of us shooting barebow, our number one pastime is hunting, not the shooting of a bow and arrow. Our preferred method of hunting is with the bow and arrow. Our preferred style of bow and arrow is barebow.

We're going to show you and tell you how to build the entire shot, but all we really can accomplish is to give you guidelines. We can give you the general outline of what you should do to shoot this style, but through the learning process and through experimentation you will adapt and fine tune the particulars to fit your body style and preferences. We are all built differently, and we all have personal likes and dislikes. You're going to have to pick and choose what fits you. For instance, the stance I recommend seems to work for most people, but it might not work well for everyone.

STANCE

Making a barebow shot is like making a shot in basketball or golf, or hitting a baseball. YOU BUILD THE SHOT FROM THE GROUND UP. Therefore, as I teach "from the ground up", I teach the stance as if you were actually stalking an animal. Make believe that the target is the live animal, that you are stalking it, and you must be able to stop and shoot quickly, if needed, and accurately always. That is the position your feet should be in when shooting a longbow from the traditional stalking stance. That simply means a right handed shooter will have the left foot forward and a left handed shooter will have the right foot forward.

Weight distribution should be centered, equally distributed on both feet. By being centered, you have, first, a stable platform to shoot from and second, much better pivoting ability for moving game or switching targets, or whatever motion may be demanded. Your feet should be as wide apart as your shoulders. The arch of the back foot must be exactly in line with the bowstring, shoulders, arrow, bow hand and a straight line to the center of the target. The forward foot is back off the line to the target but pointed toward the target. Please note the illustration on page 16.

With proper form, your drawing arm elbow, at full draw, will be directly over the arch of the right foot (for a right handed shooter). That's why I call it the anchor foot.

Pivoting? If the target is moving from right to left, I pivot on the left (front) foot. If the target is moving left to right, I pivot on the right (back) foot. This is the easiest, surest way to maintain balance

● *Good, consistent shooting form means putting the pieces together, from the ground up. Just remember that everyone is physically different, so once you have the basics, you'll have to fine-tune to your personal needs and preferences. It is intended that you use the main photo on this page as a reference point for what follows in this chapter, plus the individual photos included with the explanations of various steps.*

16

with maximum maneuverability. Remember that I'm a right hand shooter. If you're a left hand shooter, just switch things.

BODY POSITION

I don't stand up straight, nor do I lock any joints. Habit has something to do with it, but it's a learned habit, and it must be a learned habit for this "become the arrow" system.

If you stand up straight, you tend to extend more like you would with a compound bow, and that doesn't work for this shooting method. Another reason for NOT standing up straight is to get your shoulders, bow arm, everything, in as exact alignment with the target as possible, **while also getting the arrow as close to directly under your eye as possible.** Also, if you get the arrow too high -- the nock too close to the bottom of your eye -- your string arm and elbow will be too high, angling upward, which causes loss of control. When you have a bow with no letoff, you just can't shoot this way. The raised drawing arm is out of the desired alignment and prevents your muscles from working properly. As an analogy, if you were trying to pull a rope, would you rather pull with your arms raised to your ears or down at chest level? Controlling the drawn bow is the same thing; with a heavier weight, you might not be able to draw it.

I bend my knees slightly. The left knee will be bent more than the right, because I'm a right handed shooter. Since my upper body is extended slightly, and I need to keep the proper balance, the left knee has to bend more than the right knee. The bent left knee also comes from hunting, from considerable shooting from a tree stand. Rather

● *The forward knee must bend slightly when shooting down out of tree stands or at any close shot. This helps keep your shoulders, bow arm, etc., in proper alignment. DO NOT bend at the waist.*

than bending from the waist to get the proper downward angle for a shot, it's easier -- and much better -- to bend at the knees, keeping your body in a normal shooting form with arms and shoulders perpendicular to your body. You will feel more comfortable; all your subconscious signals will still be right; your draw length will remain the right length, and you will make a better shot. When you bend at the forward knee, you're simply less likely to drop your bow arm. A dropped bow arm is what shortens your draw length and leads to all sorts of changes, none of them good. Anything you can do to keep your bow arm perpendicular to your body, do it.

If the target is below you, bend the forward knee to tilt your body; if the target is uphill, bend your back knee. Also, when you're standing on the ground, shooting at close targets, such as 10 steps, the target is sharply below you, so you will need to bend the forward knee. But with targets 20, 30 and further steps, you won't need to bend either knee as much.

BREATH CONTROL

What you want to do is lower the center of gravity. Bending the knees will do some of this. The Oriental belief is that the soul is centered in the abdomen, therefore the Zen masters teach students to breathe by dropping the diaphragm and expanding the abdomen rather than the chest. (This is the same way singers breathe.) Whether or not it actually lowers the center of gravity, it works. You have the sensation of a lowered center of gravity, giving you better balance.N o w bring the bowstring back to anchor. Once you hit the anchor, continue to pull by pushing your elbow back. Many people will stop drawing here, but that is wrong. If you do that, your string hand elbow will project almost at right angle to the bowstring. You've got to keep your back muscles involved. They will help pull your elbow in line with the arrow shaft and the target.

Here's where the second benefit of this type of abdominal breath control occurs. Once everything is lined up....the elbow is back and you're continuing the drawing tension (you never stop pulling the bowstring)....inhale more to fill your lungs. Then allow the air you're holding low to come up into your chest. Your chest will expand, forcing your string arm back just a little more. The back muscles are pulling your string arm; the chest muscles feel like they're pushing your string arm. This helps you to continue drawing the bowstring....just a little bit, but enough to continue positive control. You get a clean release. It prevents string plucking, helps the bow arm stay rock steady.

That's the difference between being an excellent shot and an ok shot.

● A solid bow arm is essential to good shooting. It will make good shooting form the best it can be, and it will forgive minor errors in other parts of your shooting form when you're having an off day. Best way to develop the thought of a solid bow arm is to think "ANCHOR the bow arm". The right handle design should force your bow hand into the same position, shot after shot.

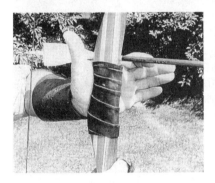

BOW HAND & BOW ARM

Everyone makes a big deal of anchoring their draw, but you have to **anchor the bow** also. You have to hold the bow on target while you aim, while you release and after you release. If you pluck the bowstring as you release, you also will throw your bow arm. It is possible to make a bad release <u>and get away with it</u>, because with the bow arm ANCHORED on target, the arrow is still going to hit the mark.

How to grip the bow? This is getting back to anchoring the bow. A lot is made of a statement Howard Hill made in his book, "Hunting The Hard Way", where he said the bow should be held as in a vise. People take that to mean you should have a death grip on the bow.

I cannot believe that is what he meant. I think what he meant was to anchor the bow and hold the bow on target as if it was in a vise. So it wouldn't move.

As to actually how to hold the bow, the bowyer himself should be able to shape the handle in such a way that you will hold the bow properly depending on how the bow is tillered and how he meant the bow to be shot. The bow handle should be shaped in such a way that it forces your hand into the same grip every time. The best we can hope for is to make it torque the same with each shot. A recurve or compound can be equipped with a stabilizer to minimize the torquing action, but a longbow cannot.

● *A low wrist grip creates a pressure "life line" from the bow grip through your hand, and directly into arm bone. This is less stress than a high wrist. Remember to use a loose grip; a tight grip creates problems and jars your teeth.*

I like a low wrist grip. It tends to put the pressure more in line with the palm, the "life line", through the center of the arm where the major bones are located. That gives me better control. It takes the stress off the wrist muscles, too. The exact pressure point on my bow hand is right at the base of my thumb in my palm.

There are two major advantages to the low wrist:
1) Better control of the bow;
2) Consistent draw length.

I don't use a tight grip, but just enough pressure in the grip to keep the bow from jumping out of my hand on release. I do NOT squeeze the handle. If the handle is gripped too tightly, you build tension into your bow arm, making you more likely to move the bow arm upon release of the bowstring. The arm can go up, down or sideways, you don't know.

A tight grip has one other nasty -- it will jar the ever living life out of you when you shoot. This -- hand shock on a bow -- is something people talk about all the time, because they've always heard that longbows were supposed to jar the fillings from your teeth. Rather than being dissipated in the bow, all the shock goes right into your bow hand, wrist and arm. No one can ever fully accept it or get used to it, and it certainly isn't something you will ever appreciate.

Also, most of the time a death grip on the bow is accompanied by a locked elbow, so there is no forward movement, no flex, in the arm at the release. When the arm is locked straight, you're creating a nice pipeline for all that shock to run right up to your teeth. With the elbow slightly bent, your muscles act as a shock absorber.

My bow arm elbow is rotated out of the way, but it is not locked. When you're shooting with an open stance, you'll find it more difficult to lock the elbow. You push forward toward the target, trying to straighten the bow arm, as far as you can without locking the elbow.

This is another reason for having everything in a straight line. If you turn with the more closed stance, with both feet positioned closer to 90 degrees to the arrow -- a style more likely to be used with a compound bow or any bow with a sighting system -- you will tend to have the elbow straighter. This would stretch you out more, closing

● *The bow arm is rotated out of the way but not locked. When shooting with an open stance, you'll find it more difficult to lock the elbow.*

your stance a bit and potentially creating clearance problems. Also, if you already have a long draw, you would have an even tougher time finding wood arrows which would spine out right.

If you go the other way and get too much bend in your bow arm, or too much of an open stance, your muscles will give out quickly and you will lose control.

Of course, it helps to have shot a lot, to have built up your shooting muscles.

BOW SHOULDER

Both shoulders should be parallel with the drawing elbow-eye-arrow-bow arm-target line. This ensures that pressure on your bow shoulder will always be in that same straight line, particularly when you're using a heavy bow. If your stance becomes too open, the pressure on your bow shoulder will shift from in-line to the front, pushing the shoulder back out of alignment. Tearing up your shoulder, in fact, and causing all sorts of physical grief.

Bow shoulder attitude also depends on the particular bow you shoot -- whether that bow is made with a low wrist grip, a medium wrist grip or high wrist grip. Few traditional bows have a high wrist grip, because the heavier holding weights put more strain on the wrist muscles than the shooter can withstand for any length of time. Accompanying that exhaustion would be loss of control. With a low or medium wrist, there's more straight-line pressure on the sinew and bone in your wrist, arm and shoulder, and less tension on the muscles in your wrist. Also, a high wrist grip has less control because the muscles required to hold the wrist high become tired.

● *Both shoulders should be parallel with the drawing elbow-eye-arrow-bow arm-target line. This ensures that pressure on your bow shoulder will always be in that same straight line, particularly when you're using a heavy bow.*

● Anchor points vary from person to person. Different anchor points are caused by different physical make-ups, different head shapes and different personal preferences. The common goal is to get the arrow exactly in line with the center of the pupil of the eye.

ANCHOR

Before getting into this point, allow me to express one frustration. This is something that absolutely amazes me. People who are knowledgeable archers, who have been in the sport for years, for some reason feel that when they pick up the traditional bow all the basics of archery go out the window. I sometimes wonder whether that then becomes a built-in and readily available excuse for them to put the traditional gear back down, saying, "Ah, I can't shoot this stuff", and return to their other archery gear.

Now....

I shoot with the bowstring in the outermost joint of the three fingers on the bowstring. I shoot split finger style, one above the nock and two below. I use the center finger at the corner of the mouth. Actually, saying "corner of the mouth" isn't quite right, because lips can move, which means an anchor at the corner of the mouth may be inconsistent.

Anchoring on the exposed tip of an upper jaw tooth is your most consistent anchor. Since your lower jaw can move, anchoring on a tooth in the lower jaw also could give an inconsistent anchor.

The upper front tip of the fingernail on my center finger hits the exposed tip, or cusp, of my second bicuspid tooth (the second one back from the canine), and that's where I stay.

Anchors will vary from individual to individual. Every shooter must realize and understand that. Different anchor points are caused by different physical make-ups, different head shapes and different personal preferences. **There is, however, a common goal -- to get the**

● *Tied in with anchor point is head angle. Your head must be in the proper position to let you look straight down the arrow shaft.*

arrow exactly in line with the center of the pupil of the aiming eye. Again, that straight line from drawing arm elbow all the way to the target. When the eye is over the arrow, that's got to be the center of the pupil.

Sight shooters often look through the string because the bow isn't canted, but sometimes their reference is the left side of the string or the right side of the string -- it doesn't matter which, as long as you're consistent -- hence, the bow is held vertically. But barebow shooters can't. We have to have our aiming eye right over the arrow so we're in line. Since our bow must be canted, the string will angle across the face, but the point where the nock of the arrow touches the string must be directly under the center of the pupil.

HEAD ANGLE

You want to get your head into position which lets you look straight down the shaft. Not slightly to one side or the other of the shaft, but right on top of the shaft so the power and sight lines are true right to the target.

Tilt your head forward and to the side at the same time. As noted in earlier segments of this chapter -- line things up before the pupil of your eye.

I've been doing it so long, I'm not even aware that I'm tilting my head. You will get to that same point.

Note: The preceding items -- Body Position, Breath Control, Bow Hand & Bow Arm, Bow Shoulder, Anchor and Head Angle -- must be learned, and learned well, to "become the arrow". Once you have them locked into your memory, your shot building efforts will speed through them and concentrate first on stance and then on Pick A Spot, which follows.

PICK A SPOT

I know you've heard "pick a spot" thousands and thousands of times. However, it's not enough to pick a spot. That spot has to be small....extremely small....the smaller the better. If you can pick out a single hair to concentrate on, do it. The reason is simple -- increased focus and concentration, the bringing of all your powers onto one small point. So if you pick a very small spot and aim at it, you might not hit that exact spot, but you will hit close enough to be well inside the kill zone.

I used to be the world's worst at what I call zone shooting on animals. Zone shooting is just trying to put the arrow somewhere in the kill zone. Normally, my arrow would end up just out of the kill zone. My focus wasn't good enough; I allowed outside things to intrude on my mental preparation.

Something my good friend Jerry Simmons taught me years ago helped me immeasurably, and it might well help you. I was reading everything I could about archery at that time. We were talking about picking an imaginary spot, and that was giving me fits. I guess I just don't have much imagination, because I could not seem to pick a spot and concentrate on it.

Jerry told me that was bull. "Look at it right and you will see a spot," Jerry said. "There will be a hair out of place, or there will be a spot of sunlight shining on that animal. There might be a wrinkle of skin, or whatever. There definitely will be something that you can see to aim at if you look hard enough."

That is one hundred percent correct, one hundred percent of the time. Even on something as uniform in marking as a black bear. There might be a fly at the right place on the bear's fur. There might be a piece of alder bark on its side. There WILL be something you can see to aim at.

● When you're picking a spot, pick the smallest spot possible. Such as a light hair on the topline of the cluster of lighter toned hairs just behind this buck's left elbow, maybe five inches up from the bottom line of its body. Or a hair on the back end of this cluster of lighter toned hairs. Photo by Troy Huffman.

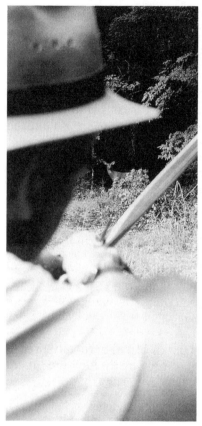

● *Canting the bow moves the top limb out of your sight picture. The right degree of cant will put your arrow where the two lines cross in your tuning target. Start with your bow fairly vertical, then keep tilting it until your arrow hits where the lines cross.*

SET THE CANT

With a longbow, there is no elevated arrow rest involved. The arrow sits on a small shelf right above your bow hand. It is close to the pivot point of the bow hand / bow unit. Since it IS closer to the pivot point, canting the bow will have a less dramatic effect on the arrow's point of impact than if you canted any bow which employs an elevated arrow rest. Even though it has less dramatic effect, the cant is not as critical with the longbow as with any bow employing an elevated rest.

There are two reasons to cant the bow:

1) It moves the top limb out of your sight picture, getting it completely over to the side where you don't even see it. This obviously lets you see the target better.

2) Get the arrow to strike on a vertical line, in effect setting your right/left alignment. This puts the windage half of your shot together. (The elevation half of your shot is decided when you visualize the arrow's flight path.) Just remember....if the arrow is flying down

26   The System

the center it stands a chance; it is if off to the right or left there is no chance for it.

How do you know how much cant to put on the bow? You shoot test arrows, changing the cant, until the arrows hit the vertical line.

Begin by holding the bow almost vertical and release an arrow. Normally, if you are a right hand shooter you will hit left and high, and if you are a left hand shooter you will hit right and high.

For the next shot, cant the bow slightly, say 10 degrees, tilting the upper limb to the right if you're a right hand shooter or to the left if you're a left hand shooter. You should see the arrow begin to 'walk' to closer to the vertical line, just like you were adjusting the settings on a rifle scope. Keep tilting the bow until your arrow hits the vertical line. That is the degree of cant you need for accurate barebow shooting.

Here's where the reason for using the center finger to anchor your draw against an upper tooth comes into play. Your top and bottom fingers will still be holding the bowstring, but they also are freed to anchor your bow's degree of cant. Place them on certain places on your face which will act as pressure points. You'll be able to feel how much the string is torquing and you will know how much the bow is canting.

If, for instance, you have the bow held too vertically, which means there isn't enough cant, you will feel excessive pressure on the top finger because the bowstring is torquing. The bowstring will torque just the opposite, putting excess pressure on your bottom finger, if you have too much cant. When you don't have the right cant, the bowstring will be trying to pull your fingers to line up with the bow.

Those "certain places" on my face are the index finger under the cheekbone under my right eye and the third finger on the line where my teeth enter the gum of my lower jaw.

VISUALIZE THE ARROW IN FLIGHT / MENTAL PROJECTION

First, while you're drawing the bow, visualize the arrow in flight.

Visualizing the flight path is a lot like throwing a ball or a rock, in that you would visualize how high you had to throw the ball/rock in order to get it on the target. Visualize the fletches spinning, the arrow dropping in and hitting perfectly. That's mental projection, and that's what you want. An unexpected benefit, the first time it happens, is that as you visualize the flight pattern you also will be able to see obstructions to your arrow's actual flight.

● *When you see the proper sight picture, your arrow tip will be out of focus at the bottom of that sight picture, as shown here in this simulated situation.*

Second, see the sight picture. The tip of the arrow will be out of focus at the bottom of this picture. It is a straight line <u>below</u> the arc of the visualized arrow in flight. This serves as a cross-reference. Don't do this step alone, because you'll miss whatever flight path obstructions exist. It's more like the split image view you'll get when focusing a camera — when they come together, you release.

These two steps obviously happen much faster than I can tell you about them.

On ordinary days you don't have the level of concentration that you will when you're shooting at a trophy buck. While practicing, you'll see the mark clearly, but not necessarily in crisp focus. When you're really humming, you will be able to see the hair splitting on the buck's rib cage as the arrow hits.

Visualizing the flight path -- its arc from bow to target -- is a form of distance judging that has proven highly reliable for me in hunting. I use it because it isn't practical to take your eye off the animal to guess the distance. I can, because of practice, recognize the sight picture -- the flight path, actually -- the arrow should take to get to the target.

When I visualize an arrow in flight, all I'm doing is bringing the bow arm up to where it hits the angle I have visualized. I can misjudge the proper arc for the arrow a little, i.e., misjudge the flight path slightly, yet the arrow seems to hit within the kill zone of the animal, whereas a misjudged distance of as little as three yards for sight pin use seems to produce a higher probability of a miss. For me, it just doesn't seem to be as critical to judge the arc as to judge the distance.

If you learn to judge the flight path the arrow must take to hit the target, rather than which sight pin to use, you will be more likely to take the animal, I believe. If you're going to use a *definite* sighting mechanism on the bow, I believe then you also will need a more *definite* distance judging system, such as a rangefinder. This will slow you down, but it may be to your advantage.

This barebow principle and practice will work with the compound bow, too. The theory and the practice aren't wedded solely to a traditional bow, but traditional is what I know the best, and that's what I'm talking about here. Jerry Simmons has proven to me quite well that a compound bow can be shot barebow effectively. He shoots off the shelf, at moving and stationary targets, effectively.

We Can't Judge Distance Like We Think We Can

I cannot judge distance well. I'm not alone in being a poor judge of distance, but I'm more willing to admit it than are most bowhunters. We all practice with our bow, but we don't practice distance judging. That's too boring.

A few years ago, we attended an eastern state bowhunting associations's fall shoot. They had a distance judging contest as sort of a novelty event, "test yourself", and all that. The ten targets included two rabbits, two turkeys, three whitetail deer, two raccoons and one black bear. The cardboard targets were life-size and lifelike. They weren't 3-D, but still....

Target distances were typical, ranging from 18 feet to 75 feet. The 10 target distances added up to 384 feet. Participants estimated the distance in feet from marker stakes to the targets, with a different stake for each target. Accuracy was determined simply by adding their 10 estimates and seeing how close they were to the actual total of the 10 distances.

Keep in mind that the participants were experienced bow shots, some more and some less. At least, though, they already were interested enough in shooting the bow and in bowhunting that they were aware of the association and its fall event, and they were interested enough in the activity to attend and then partici-

VISUALIZING FOR QUARTERING SHOTS

Some bowhunters, to achieve the desired results -- especially on quartering shots -- will focus on the *exit* point of the arrow instead of the entry point. By focusing where they want the arrow to exit, they know the arrow will have to go through the vital area in the deer. The exact point of exit is unseen, but they can concentrate on it so well, envision it so well, that it becomes clear and in focus in their mind's eye.

Another way to look at it, and the method I prefer, is to visualize a basketball in the deer's chest. No matter what angle from me the animal is standing, I shoot for the center of the basketball. The basketball doesn't change positions, only the deer's body changes. The basketball visualization functions as an enlarged pivot point and thus is the center of focus.

MR. HOWARD HILL AND HIS "SPLIT VISION" STYLE

Mr. Hill bent at the waist, kind of hunched his shoulders forward and bent his knees. What he was concerned with was getting all the angles correct, where the tip of the arrow is pointed at what he was seeing with his aiming eye, which was right over the arrow shaft,

pate in the distance judging. You would naturally conclude, then, that they were more attuned to distance judging simply because they most likely practice it more often than the average bow shooter.

If that is so, then the results show just how far off the person who DOESN'T shoot much probably will be. For these people didn't do all that wonderfully, either.

Here's the distance-estimate list of 26 people who tried their skills at distance judging. These are totals, in feet, of their estimates for 10 targets:

284, 297, 304, 344, 364, 365, 369, 377, 393, 395, 402, 407, 410, 416, 423, 432, 441, 444, 450, 456, 457, 460, 468, 501, 537, 543.

Remember that the actual total was 384 feet.

Only seven were within 20 feet, plus or minus, of the actual total. That's only two feet off per target, yet sometimes that little bit can mean a lot of difference. Average target distance was 38.4 feet. Dividing the two-foot average estimating error by 38.4 gives a 5.21 percentage error.

The bow is a slow hunting tool. The arrow has more arc in the trajectory than we often realize. There just isn't much margin for error regarding distance judging when we use the bow.

It's interesting that eight people judged short and 18 judged and with the proper gap between arrow tip and center of the target. He also was concerned with his draw length. All his physical adaptations served to shorten his draw, because he needed to. He was concerned with arrow spine. He shot heavy, heavy draw weights. He need a shorter arrow to get the necessary spine without going to some incredible arrow shaft weights and diameters....telephone poles.

In his formative years, there simply wasn't anything available but wood arrows. Aluminum arrow shafts didn't become available until later in his career. He realized early that the longer draw was a severe detriment to him. Because he was a big man, and if he extended the way we would shoot most bows today, he would have had a 32-inch draw, or close to it. By bending at the waist, bending over at the shoulders, hunching the shoulders forward a little bit, bending his knees, shooting with a slightly crooked bow arm, he got down to a 28-inch draw.

Mr. Hill's "split vision" method of aiming was basically gap shooting. The exception is, because of the equipment he had available, in his peripheral vision he would see the arrow not only well below the mark but also to the right of the mark. Why? Because the bows he shot were not even close to being center shot. They had a

---

long. In fact, the longest estimate was more than five yards off, on average, per target. That wouldn't have been the case on the shorter shots at rabbits, so you can imagine how far off the longer distance estimates would be. All estimates were made from the ground.

We all know the general mistake is to shoot high on game, either because we get excited and just don't concentrate enough, or we overestimate the distance. It's been proven time and again that deer aren't as large in body size as we generally believe they are. So when that factor is combined with what appears to be a distance judging problem, it's easy to see why we shoot high frequently. It may be painful to admit that we aren't always that good at judging distances, but we are not that good. Especially when you add factors such as excitement of the hunt, an approaching animal (maybe of large size or with large antlers), combinations of shadows and light which intensify or decrease light, the relatively unfamiliar setting and related lack of confirmed reference points and the somewhat unfamiliar perspective of the view from a treestand.

Several Army studies of gunnery and infantry personnel have confirmed that the human animal is nowhere near as good a judge of distance as he thinks he is.

tiny little shelf on which to rest the arrow, nothing more. No attempt was made to move the arrow more toward the center line of the bow because the bow would break. The available materials were not strong enough to withstand the larger degree of cutout. This extremely off-center arrow placement caused extreme archer's paradox.

My barebow shooting style began to develop when I was attempting to learn Mr. Hill's split vision method of aiming. Following Mr. Hill's explanations, my arrows were hitting the target inconsistently. I worked on this a couple of years without much luck. At that time I didn't have enough knowledge and insight to understand Mr. Hill's explanation of his system.

When I began to understand why I couldn't duplicate his method, I began making headway. First, I realized the effect of head shape on your anchor. (This is one of the more valuable points you must remember when finding your proper anchor point.) To get the arrow lined up right in front of the pupil of his eye, Mr. Hill anchored on the last tooth of his lower jaw. When I tried that anchor point, the arrow nock was to the right of my eye pupil. I had to anchor farther forward to position the arrow directly under the pupil of my eye. I finally realized that Mr. Hill had a longer, narrower head shape than I do.

Then I began to understand that the more modern materials and styling of today's traditional archery equipment, while looking much the same as what Mr. Hill used, are vastly different and better. My bows today, equipped with Fast Flite bowstrings, will shoot a 650 grain arrow out of a 70 pound bow at approximately 200 feet per second. That's faster than the original compound bows would shoot.

The modern materials I mean are uni-directional fiberglass for facing and backing, biased glass materials for bow cores, phenolic overlays for limb tips, Fast-Flite (Kevlar) materials for strings, and newer serving materials on the bowstrings. Because of these modern bow building components, we are able to make our bows centershot, if desired. Most traditional bowyers, including myself, will still leave the sight window a minimum of 1/8-inch off center. We leave it off center to meet the requirement for longbows in archery tournaments.

Because of aluminum and graphite arrows, and of course the bowstrings, we can don't need to shorten our draw lengths as Mr. Hill did. All we need to do is build a bow and some arrows to fit our draw length. Centershot is a related factor because it lessens archer's paradox and therefore the wider range of spines and weights of arrows can be used.

While attempting to learn the split vision method of aiming, I learned that by the cant of the bow and my more- forward anchor point, the "imaginary spot" Mr. Hill was talking about, that he aimed his arrow at, and the spot I aimed at with my more modern gear were one and the same. All I had to do was look at the spot I wanted to hit and fire at it. He called it the split vision method of aiming. I call it gap shooting.

"Become the arrow" goes beyond all of this. *Gap shooting is nothing more than having the ability to focus on the spot you want to hit, while at the same time seeing the arrow out of the bottom of your peripheral vision.* You'll be aware of that arrow just like you were pointing your finger. You're aware of where it is in relation to that aiming cross, but you're not concentrating on it. You're concentrating on the juncture of the two lines. If you ever let your eyes wander from the spot to be hit to the arrow, let down, because the gap system won't work like that. You have to remain focused on the spot you want to hit.

If everything is right, you release, and now you have a reference. You know where that first arrow hit. You know where it was pointing in relation to the aiming cross. Your second shot should be in the cross or close to it. Mr. Hill used to say that anyone has an excuse for missing the first shot, but no one has an excuse for missing twice.

Once you begin learning this method of shooting, it is easy to be accurate at 10 to 15 steps. It's not so easy to be accurate at 20 to 30 steps or beyond. That's when gap shooting comes into play. When you move farther from the target, you have to pay even more attention to detail. In the beginning, you're going to have to really think about the proper size of the gap. As you progress in skill level, it will be no harder to shoot accurately at 20 paces than at 10. The same applies as you progress farther and farther out.

Unfortunately, most shooters stop progressing when they become competent with the gap shooting method....and that's what trips them up.

Imagine a deer hunting situation. It's getting dark. A deer in light cover exposes its rib cage. Is it 20 paces or 30 paces? You're at full draw....can you see the gap? Probably not, yet the difference in 10 paces means 10 inches in gap. Also, your arrow now has a broadhead tip, rather than the field point you're accustomed to seeing in practice. The broadhead is more difficult to pick up in your peripheral vision.

Don't become too dependent on gap shooting. Once you have become proficient, immediately begin concentrating more on the mark and less on the gap. This will begin your refinement of the clear focus aspect mentioned in the introduction, and this sets you on the road to becoming the arrow. When you become the arrow, you visualize the arrow's flight path in the above deer hunting situation, you cross-reference it with the sight picture, you pick a spot behind the deer's shoulder and release. It doesn't matter whether the deer is 20 or 30 paces. In gap shooting, you have to estimate the range and be relatively accurate. But with the "become the arrow" system, hunting distance estimation is not a determining factor in the shot.

The gap obviously changes with distance. "Point on" is putting the point of the arrow on the spot to be hit on the target. With broadheads, since they are physically longer, you will see the point of the broadhead. If you are using field points, the shoulder of the point would look to be touching the spot on the target to be hit. There's really not that much difference.

My "point on" is 60 paces. The gap between arrow tip and target spot will be below the spot at any distance less than 60 paces, and above the spot at any distance greater than 60 paces. In fact, the gap for 70 paces would be the same as the gap for 10 paces, but above the target instead of below it. The gap for 80 paces would be the same as for 20 paces, but above the target. And so on.

The gap actually is bounded top and bottom by two different lines, and you have to have the gap between them the right size for the specific shot distance so the line down the arrow directed to the target and the line from your eye directed to the target converge at the target.

● *"Point on" means putting the point of the arrow on the spot to be hit on the target. Ferguson's "point on" is at 60 paces The sight picture gap obviously changes with distance changes. At less than "point on", the arrow tip will be below the target; at distances greater than "point on", the arrow tip will be above the target.*

I'm not advocating shooting at game beyond 60 yards, but now and then you may. How do you figure the gap if your fist and the bow handle are in the way? The best way is to learn to look through your bow hand and bow handle. By keeping both eyes open, you can do this. One eye will be blocked but the other will see past the obstruction. Together, they make it appear to your brain that you are looking through your hand.

Gap sighting is something you learn. Once you've got it, you've got it. Things will change, however, if you change to a bow with a different draw weight or if you change arrows. Keeping your brain, in the heat of the moment, from messing up and flashing back to the old gap could be a big problem. That's the reason I shoot the same weight bow during exhibitions and when hunting, so I won't need to learn a new gap.

However, **the gap can be a constant.** For instance, if a person wants to shoot a 70-pound draw weight traditional bow but his muscles can't yet handle that weight, he can begin increasing bow weight and ADJUSTING ARROW LENGTH until he reaches his goal -- without changing his gap. It's a matter of shooting, of figuring out the length the arrow will have to be.

This can work in the other direction, too. For instance, you're accustomed to shooting a 60 pound bow, but you break your arm and can shoot only 45 pounds after the cast comes off. To maintain the same gap, you must find an arrow shaft which will be a proper spine for the 45 pounds and significantly longer than the arrow you're accustomed to shooting. Just how much longer can be determined only through trial and error.

SET THE PACE

This may be something you have not heard, but it is true, and it is important. It means that if the arrow is drawn quickly you should shoot quickly; if drawn slowly, be slow to release it. This is the RHYTHM OF THE SHOT. It's easy to remember that if you draw it fast shoot it fast, and if you draw it slow, shoot it slow.

RELEASE

Go to any archery tournament and all the finger shooters there, whether shooting traditional or compound, are griping about their release. They wish their release was better, or they have a sloppy release. I'm just as bad as everyone else. But if you'll hold that bow arm still, the release ISN'T GOING TO MATTER MUCH.

Release is a bad term. I don't particularly like it. "Release" means that we have to do something, that there is a motion or a job to be done. In reality, all we are doing is to quit holding the bowstring.

● *"Release" isn't a properly descriptive term. Actually, you simply quit holding the string and let the string push your fingers out of the way. It — the release — is a stopping of action, rather than an action. Ferguson advises you learn to release your whole body side. You will find that your arrows will fly better and faster with a super clean release.*

We don't do anything; we quit doing something. We cannot mentally throw those three fingers open fast enough to clear the string cleanly. The best we can hope for is to relax the fingers and let string push them out of the way.

There have been any number of ways talked about or written about as to just how does one accomplish that. Most common advice is to relax the back of the hand, which is a good start. Some instructors advise relaxing the hand and forearm, which is better. I suggest you learn to RELEASE YOUR WHOLE BODY SIDE. This is something you may not have heard much about. You will find that your arrows will fly better and much faster. Your releases will be more consistent.

You will know you have accomplished this when the fingers of your release hand touch your shoulder on the release side. You know then that you have relaxed that whole side.

Chapter 3
PRACTICE -- SHOOTING FORM

When you're working on form, that's the ONLY thing you should be working on. Worry later about grouping and hitting the middle of the target.

Set up a big target butt (I use a three-foot by two-foot bag) and **stand three steps** from it. Close your eyes and concentrate on the particular aspect of your shooting form you want to strengthen. Isolate whatever it is needs work -- anchoring the bow, anchoring the release, getting the elbow back, whatever -- making sure you work on only one item at a time.

Then **shoot** from three steps with your eyes closed. You MUST shoot an arrow. You stand only three steps from the target so you don't have to be concerned about missing the target.

At three steps, you can almost touch the target butt with the arrow. That's really all you need be concerned about....just to be far enough from the target that the arrow will clear the bow when you release.

Shoot only one arrow. Pull it and shoot again. Pulling it is easy; all you do is take one step forward.

You could really bury an arrow in a target butt at that close distance, so use the right material to prevent that. The butt I use is a woven flat plastic fiber bag stuffed with a cotton-like material. This type of butt stops the arrow but does not grip it. You can pull the

● When you practice, work on shooting form. Worry later about grouping and the middle of the bullseye. Set up a big target butt and stand three steps from it. Close your eyes and concentrate on the particular part of your shooting form you want to improve.

arrow with two fingers. Nor will the arrow shoot through. The arrow may kick up, down, left or right with a target this soft, but it doesn't matter. The target is suspended at the upper corners, but it also has a ground anchor so it won't swing.

How much to practice on a specific part of your shooting form? For as long as you feel comfortable.

People are fond of quoting Mr. Hill on this topic. He said that he did shoot 50 arrows a day, working on nothing but form. He was quite concerned with appearance. At that time, he was shooting for the movies, so he had to look good.

Actually, he would shoot 144 arrows a day, 50 of which were dedicated solely to working on his shooting form. But that doesn't mean he shot 144 arrows at once. He was a busy man, writing, working on bows and what have you. He kept a dozen arrows at the back door of his house and a dozen arrows at the door of his shop. Any time he was going from one to the other, he would shoot a dozen arrows.

I shoot only three arrows at a time. That's all I can shoot and maintain the desired level of concentration. Practice must have quality. Volume practice doesn't accomplish much other than building stamina and muscle power; on the negative side, volume practice could create and establish bad habits. When we're tired, we're lazy and sloppy. So, when practicing, it is important we know our mental limit; it almost always occurs before we reach our physical limit.

The standard commentary is that you really shoot only one arrow. This is the absolute truth. You don't make five shots; you shoot one arrow five times. There is only one shot, and you learn from each one. You forget the bad things from one arrow, from one shot. You go to the next shot, reinforcing in your mind the good things from the previous shot.

You build on strength, but you practice your weak points. Most people want to practice their strong points, because they feel better and enjoy it more. They don't want to practice their weak points because that's work and possibly discouraging. The applicable cliche here: A chain is only as strong as its weakest link. Your shooting skills are only as strong as the weakest element of your shooting form.

If you can shoot only one arrow a day, but concentrate with full focus on that one arrow, I believe it will do you more good than shooting 100 arrows. You reach a point where the shooting repetitiveness becomes mindless. You're like a machine, and a machine can't think or retrain itself. Your goal is to develop the feel, mentally and physically, of a perfect shot, to building muscle "memory" and the subconscious controls and recognition points. But don't go one shot beyond your limit in building those positive references.

There is a joy in the development of that muscle memory, that feel. There is subconscious control, the result of training, but it feels as if it is almost totally a physical thing, for when it happens your entire body feels right, feels in harmony, feels smooth and in command. You KNOW that what is about to happen will happen perfectly, and your conscious mind and "outer" senses can enjoy the action as it happens. Sometimes it seems like you're watching yourself perform, and you're getting thrilled -- and deeply satisfied -- by the performance as it builds and as it happens. It's like a river flow-ing, the fluidity, smoothness and continuity of it all. It truly can be a spiritual experience.

To have quality concentration, your mind cannot wander. You must have full concentration on the object in question, whether that be a part of your form, practicing with your eyes shut, or whether that be the target as you try to bring the center of the bullseye into sharp focus for the shot. You certainly can't be wondering about the next shot, or about a piece of your shooting equipment.

PHYSICAL EXERCISES

If you're just getting into traditional archery, a bull worker -- a spring activated item -- is great for practicing drawing. It definitely will help physical buildup of the right muscles. It's like drawing and anchoring a bow much heavier than the bow you plan to shoot.

MENTAL EXERCISES

Mental exercises consist mostly of always trying to pick the smallest aiming spot possible on anything you look at. For example, when you look at a stop sign, look at the center of the O in the word, don't look just at the O. When you're talking to a person, look at the pupil of their eye, not just their face and eye.

● To improve your focus and concentration in picking the smallest spot possible, with a stop sign, for instance, look at the center of the O, don't look just at the O.

Shoot mental arrows, too. Look at an object and visualize an arrow in flight, hitting the exact aiming spot.

Visualization is a common practice among athletic champions. They see themselves performing well (the actual performance, not an award presentation). When they actually do it, because they've visualized it happening, it's like they're doing it a second time. Deja vu all over again.

For shooting, you don't want a lot of physical -- or mental -- tension. You want to be relaxed but controlled. There's no other way to describe it. You're good at it, and you know it. From the mental aspect of it, you know you can do the shot, you're going to do the shot, but you're not going to get all that upset if you don't. It's only one shot. If you're going to get all bent out of shape, that means you have lost mental control of your shooting.

In practice, it's important always to challenge yourself. When you first start shooting, the challenge might be just to hit a 10-inch bullseye at 10 steps. As you progress, you MUST move to smaller and smaller targets at longer and longer distance, and then to moving targets.

When you stop challenging yourself, that's as good as you'll ever be.

MUSCLE MEMORY

You get to a certain point where your body as well as your mind knows that the shot setup and visualization are right. You have implanted the feel of a good shot. Consequently, there doesn't seem to be a conscious decision to release. It just happens. Your mind and muscles have been trained to certain cues, visual and physical (covering the sight picture, visualization of the arrow flight path and physical preparation of your shooting form), and when the proper combination of those cues come together in your subconscious or inner mind or whatever you want to call it, the fingers quit holding the bowstring.

As a related example, how many times have you had a deer cross the road in front of you while you were driving your car and you tried to miss the deer? You don't think about what you're doing, you just react. You've been driving physically, with your mind reasonably well involved, but the subconscious command and physical response happen so fast you don't seem to have run it through your conscious brain, that part of the brain which doesn't recognize and process commands as quickly as the trained, subconscious. The learned things which we commit to mental and muscle memory, with the signals buried way deep, serve us well in time of need.

There is no doubt whatsoever that various parts of our brain act and react at speeds faster than other, more thought-involved parts....and act independently of the thought-involved parts. That's what allows us to miss that deer and say "whew" afterward, or which allows us to swing on a running target, shoot and down it without needing to tell ourselves "20 yards, lead by x-number feet".

It's difficult to explain, but there is a muscle memory. Or some memory buried so deep in the brain that the commands can completely bypass the thought process, kind of like a mouse scooting from under the cabin cabinet and out the door without being seen.

Sometimes arrows have a way of getting away like that. But they shouldn't. They get away like that when you're not in control, when you're not concentrating enough. You may _think_ you are, but you aren't. You can fool yourself; you can lie to yourself.

On the other hand, sometimes a setup doesn't feel right. Your command-level mind may want to do one thing, but your muscles want to do something else, or nothing at all. Or maybe your muscles are trained to respond to some silent, unthought command, but your brain overrides that signal and you don't release the arrow. If we work with the various levels of our physical, conscious and subconscious self, we have a beautiful built-in system of checks and balances.

When the would-be shot doesn't feel right, we let down, re-organize our approach and draw again. This is common on the target range, but it is equally as important in bowhunting. If it doesn't feel right, you won't make a good shot. In bowhunting, that might mean not making the shot at all. I know, I know .... you can't put brown on the ground unless you get an arrow in the air, but there are circumstances above and beyond that with each shot.

Can you manipulate your arm and body muscles to make a shot happen? Sure, but you don't "manipulate" them. They're already trained. Manipulating implies conscious, planned action. There are people who shoot a bow that way at tournament targets, but that's not the way we shoot at moving targets in a hunting situation. You don't have time for a thought process.

A rabbit jumps from beneath a brush pile and runs right across in front of me, just like it ought to. There's no way I can tell myself "That rabbit is 20 steps away, running wide open, I'd better lead it about 15 feet." That's what I do, but I don't consciously think about it until after the shot -- usually while I'm retrieving my arrow from a grass clump that _doesn't_ include the rabbit. But I sure scared the heck out of it. I try to remember how much I led the rabbit, what the picture looked like when I released, and how accurate that mental picture was.

One morning I passed up a shot at a walking doe at just less than 20 paces. I didn't feel that I could make a good shot on her, that I'd either miss or wound her. Yet, late that afternoon, I killed a running buck at 47 paces. The difference? I had not shot for a couple of days prior to the morning hunt, but during mid-day I'd practiced and done well, got myself mentally and physically grooved again, reinforced my confidence. When I swung on that running buck, it never entered my mind that I could miss. I _knew_ I was going to take that deer, take it cleanly. My arrow hit both lungs. The deer went about 30 yards.

42 Shooting Form

Chapter 4
Tuning For Barebow

There obviously isn't as much to tune on a barebow shooting setup, which is the way you want it, but there ARE things to do. And you must have the equipment tuned before you start building the basics of "become the arrow". Otherwise, it will never happen because it can't happen. GIGO (Garbage In / Garbage Out) applies here.

First, of course, is to have the arrow matched to the bow weight *at the draw weight and draw length you will be shooting.* Remember that your draw length will shorten one-and-a-half to two inches from your compound bow draw length when you switch to a longbow, because of the handle difference and because you will shoot from a more-open stance. The exact change depends upon how much you change your shooting form and how close you are to being over-bowed. Much of the change occurs simply in the way you hold the longbow versus how you hold the compound bow.

Your draw length won't shorten as much when you switch to a recurve from a compound because modern recurves USUALLY have the same riser/handle style as their compound counterparts. Recurves have a much higher brace height than a longbow. Understand me here....I'm saying that the potential draw length change of switching from compound to recurve is almost nil if you don't change your shooting form/style. However, the PRACTICAL change will be an inch or more, simply because you won't be able to handle the same peak draw weight. If you've been shooting a 70 pound compound, you'll be severely over-bowed trying to shoot a 70 pound recurve.

● *Tuning begins with proper brace height, left photo. Start with the manufacturer's recommended brace height. There is a leeway available, which lets you adjust for lighter or heavier arrows, depending upon your needs and preferences. Your draw length will shorten when you switch from a compound to traditional gear, most likely shortening more if you switch to a longbow than to a recurve.*

BRACE HEIGHT

This is where you begin tuning a longbow or recurve.

The manufacturer should have listed in his literature the recommended brace height of the bow. That number should have a variable, a minimum and maximum recommendation, but you begin tuning in the mid-range of these given variables. Some longbows, however, will carry as low as a five-inch brace height. Some bowyers will void their warranty if you shoot their bow with more than a 5-1/2 inch brace height. On the bows I manufacture, recommended brace height generally is 6-1/4 inches to 6-3/4 inches. I prefer the higher brace height because the bowstring won't slap your wrist as hard. You will be less likely to flinch from it. (It <u>will</u> sting, even through a heavy arm guard.) Bows of my manufacture are designed to be shot with the higher brace height.

The reason for the variance in recommended brace height is to give you leeway in the arrows you choose. Generally, the lighter the arrow, the higher the brace height will be, and the heavier the arrow, the lower the brace height. The lower the brace height, the longer the power stroke; therefore, with heavier arrows you will need and can use a longer power stroke delivering more energy because the arrow can handle it.

Adjust the brace height by twisting or untwisting the string. If you have a Flemish splice bowstring, twist it counter-clockwise to shorten and clockwise to lengthen. If you have a continuous-loop string, you can twist or untwist it either way to get the desired length.

BARE SHAFT TUNING

Let's say you have a 65-pound bow and a 28-inch drawn length. The recommended aluminum shaft for that bow would be a 2216. Leave the bare shaft significantly longer than your draw. Cut the bare shaft to 31 inches, for example, measured from the throat of the nock to the end of the shaft.

All test shooting will be from 10 paces.

We want the arrow to show that it is weak in spine starting out. You will know it is by the angle it sticks in the target. For a right hand shooter, the nock will be left of the arrow point; for a left hand shooter, the nock will be right of the arrow point.

Bring the spine to proper stiffness by shortening the shaft in 1/4-inch increments, testing each length, until the bare shaft sticks reasonably straight in the target. That is the proper arrow length.

ADJUST THE NOCKING POINT

Rather than use a clamp-on nocking point locator on my bowstring, I wind several loops of Fast-Flite material over the serving and tie it snug but not tight. I can twist that unit up and down the serving. This, too, is a tuning device. I start out with that adjustable lump of Fast-Flite or Dacron string positioned so the bottom of the nock will be 1/8-inch above 90 degrees.

I twist that wound-on lump of string up and down until I find the right nocking point location. At 10 paces, the bare shaft should stick in the target reasonably straight, maybe a little tail high, but definitely not more than 1-1/2 inches, and definitely not below horizontal at all.

When I locate the sweet spot as I tune, a drop of glue on that wound-on string locks it in place.

Easton Aluminum found, through high speed photography, that with only one nocking point locator, positioned above the nock, an occasional arrow will be pushed down the string and thus fly erratically. The way to stop this, of course, is to use two nocking point locators, one above and one below the nock. This will ensure that all your arrows fly the same, all other things being equal.

SHOOT A FLETCHED SHAFT

Shoot a fletched shaft cut the same length as the test bare shaft, with the same nock, same weight insert and head., The arrow should fly perfectly. If it doesn't fly perfectly, you have fletch interference.
To eliminate fletch interference, rotate the nock on the shaft. This simply moves the positions of the fletches so they will clear the shelf as they spin.

SUPER-FINE TUNING

You may find that, at longer ranges, the same shaft which flew perfectly at 10 paces will fishtail or porpoise or barrel roll. This happens because, as the arrow loses energy, imperfections in fine tuning become evident. Therefore, super-fine tuning becomes necessary.
Shoot at a minimum of 20 paces.
1) Adjust brace height again to make the shaft fly true. If the fletched shaft is striking to the right of the center of the target (right hand shooter), the spine is weak. A weak spined shaft from a left hand shot will strike to the left of center. Increase the brace height to solve this problem. If the shaft is showing slightly stiff (striking to the side of center opposite the above), decrease the brace height until the shaft flies true.
If the arrow still shows slightly weak spine, but you're at the limits of brace height to remain within warranty, add string silencers. The nearer toward the served center of the string the silencers are attached, the slower the bow will shoot, and thus the more dramatically the arrow spine will be affected. If the string silencers make the arrow fly too stiff, you can bring it back down to the proper spine by trimming the string silencers. This minutely reduced weight will let the bow shoot just enough faster to make the correction.
2) If you've done all this and the arrow still isn't quite true -- it's minnowing instead of big-fishtailing -- the pressure point where the arrow actually touches the shelf can be adjusted forward or back. The closer to the back of the bow (the side away from you), the weaker the arrow will be. The closer to the belly of the bow (the side toward you), the stiffer the arrow will be.
3) You also can change point weight to change the arrow spine. Increased point weight weakens the arrow; decreased point weight stiffens it.
4) Arrow shaft balance. FOC (Forward of Center).
a. Balance Point: Find the balance point of the arrow, with point attached, and mark that point on the shaft.
b. Center Point on Shaft:

Aluminum arrows--Measure the shaft only, from the bottom of the nock slot to the cut length of the shaft. This DOES NOT include the insert flange.

Shaft with outserts--Measure from the bottom of the nock slot to the back end of the outsert and add 3/4 inch.

Arrows with taper on front end--Measure from the bottom of the nock slot to the end of the full diameter of the shaft, the point at which the shaft begins to taper.

Mark the center of the shaft length. This mark will be behind the balance point.

The length of the shaft divided into the difference between the two marks gives you the proper FOC location for the balance point.

FOC will not affect arrow flight in terms of the trueness of the shot, but it will affect the stability of the arrow, with a secondary effect of higher retained energy down range. The general thinking is: 10% to 15% FOC is the best balance point for greatest arrow in-flight stability.

An example:

1) The shaft measures 30 inches from base of the nock slot to the cut length. Centerline therefore is 15 inches.

2) The balance point of the arrow, including point, is 1-3/4 inch forward of the centerline.

3) FOC: 1.75 / 15 = 11.5%. This is acceptable.

Arrows properly matched and tuned almost always are within the 10%-15% FOC. If your arrow does not fall within that range, and you are concerned about retained energy (for maximum broadhead penetration), you'll probably have to re-tune or start over with arrow selection and/or broadhead selection.

The heavier the arrow point, the farther forward FOC will be on the shaft. Therefore, if the FOC is greater than 15%, try a lighter weight point. If the FOC is less than 10%, try a heavier point. If the changed point weight produces an FOC within the recommended percentages AND YOUR ARROWS STILL FLY TRUE, you've solved the problem -- if you viewed it as a problem in the first place. If the arrows don't fly true, then you may have to try a different shaft length or size. First, though, tuning adjustments may solve the issue, especially if the changed point weight appears to have affected arrow flight minimally.

TROUBLE SHOOTING

You've done all the tuning and super-fine tuning, but you're still having arrow flight problems. Here's the checklist:

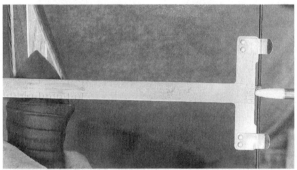
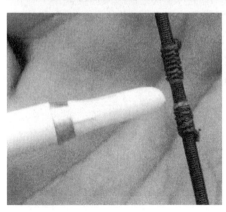

● *Various aspects of set-up, tuning and super-fine tuning: Checking nock tightness and alignment, upper left photo; checking limb tiller, upper right; nocking point height, left middle; and nocking point location firmed up with double references, so your arrow cannot slip down the string. All covered in detail in the text.*

1) String Type

Fast-Flite string will deliver more energy to the arrow than will Dacron. Therefore, Fast-Flite will make an arrow act weaker than will Dacron.

2) Nock tightness and alignment

The nock must fit on the string tight enough to hold itself on, but not so tight that it will hold the bow on. (See the photo.) Since Fast-Flite material is smaller in diameter than Dacron, the arrow nock which works well with Fast-Flite will fit too tightly on Dacron. A nock that is too tight will cause a patternless erratic arrow flight. Arrows simply won't act the same. A nock that is too loose also will cause erratic flight, but the variances won't be as dramatic.

Proper nock alignment is critical to arrow flight. Alignment devices are available commercially, any of which work fairly well. Easton's uni-bushings and Super Nock eliminate alignment problems. However, the throat of the Super Nock is so small that you MUST use Fast-Flite when a 16-strand or larger Dacron would be required.

3) Limb tiller

I read an article recently in which the writer said there was no such thing as an untuneable bow. This guy obviously never has tried

● *String silencers can be added to slow down the bow, with super-fine tuning accomplished by shortening the rubber legs of the silencers. An inconsistent grip will cause inconsistent shooting. If the grip wasn't formed to fit your hand structure and preferences, adjust it by adding and shaping material.*

to tune a longbow that was out of tiller.

Tillering of the bow refers to the strength of the limbs in relationship to one another. It is measured in fractions of an inch which denote how much closer the bottom limb is to the bowstring at the fade-out (point where the riser fades into the limb) than is the top limb at the upper fade-out. We don't hold the bow in its vertical center; we're below center. With that hand position on the bow, and the arrow position, the bottom limb must be stronger so, upon release, the timing and energy delivery of the limbs is correct. Almost always the bottom limb must be stronger than the top limb. If the bow is not tillered heavy on the bottom limb, then it is next to impossible to tune.

If you're shooting split finger method, proper tiller will be 3/16 inch to 1/4 inch. If you're shooting three-fingers-under, zero tiller to 1/8 inch will work best, because you're applying more pressure to the bottom limb, pulling back farther, making it stronger and thereby requiring less tiller.

4) Grip

An inconsistent grip, i.e., hand position on the grip, will cause inconsistent shooting. Hopefully, your bowyer has formed the grip properly to fit your hand structure and preferences. If not, you may adjust the grip by adding material, such as leather, to the heel or the throat for a better fit. Plastic wood also will work to reform the grip, but it's more work.

5) Wood arrows

This is a special situation. We're going to assume your wood arrows have been properly spined and weighed for your bow. This is difficult today because of the lack of quality wood for arrow building. The spine - great variations. The weight - great variations. The grain of the wood often twists around the shaft, causing the shaft to be crooked. Again, we're assuming you don't have those problems, but you're still getting inconsistent arrow flight.

Check to make sure the nocks are all aligned with the grain of the wood. It doesn't make any difference whether that alignment is open or closed (with the grain or across the grain); just be sure they're aligned the same.

BROADHEADS VS. FIELD POINTS

A big thing is often made of tuning with broadheads to be sure your hunting broadheads will fly where they're supposed to, because field points supposedly will group differently from broadheads. That may be true with other bows and shooting styles, but I haven't found much difference in point of impact between field points and broadheads shot from my longbow.

ALTITUDE AFFECT ON TUNING

This is an incidental thing, but it could be important to you on a Western hunt, and that's why I mention it.

The first time I hunted at higher altitudes, I discovered that I had to re-tune my bow. It didn't shoot like it did when I had tuned it, just a few days before, at the lower altitude of my Alabama home. My arrows were wild. There was no pattern, no grouping.

I missed a standing mule deer at 40 yards. I'm talking about not even alarming the deer. It was a horrendous miss by at least 20 feet. It didn't have much for antlers, so I know it wasn't buck fever. I was in good physical shape and well rested.

The deer actually walked closer. At about 20 steps, I missed low and left by a wide margin again. There was no reason for it, because when I left Alabama I was hitting two-pound plastic margarine containers two out of three times at 60 yards. With the same bow and arrow combination.

The same thing happened on the target range later that day. We have a 3-D animal target that we carry with us to practice on during such trips, and that afternoon I made the brace height change

● Contrary to wishful thinking, Western game areas aren't over-run with trophy animals, and hunting is a lot more difficult than finding a pretty place on the mountain and shooting something there. These conditions are truest when you travel infrequently to hunt new territory. So you do what you can and take what you can get and work to learn the territory and the hunting techniques so maybe next time your chances, and luck, will be better for the wall-hanger.

and switched arrows.

I talked to Norb Mullaney, the archery technician and technical advisor to the Archery Manufacturers and Merchants Organization. He said it was due mainly to the effect of the humidity and temperature changes affecting the wood in the bow and the wood arrows I was planning to use. That's another reason I started shooting aluminum exclusively.

I actually had to lower the brace height, which meant I was increasing the cast of the bow. The longer power stroke stores more energy. I don't understand that, because you would think that in the thinner air of higher altitudes, the opposite would have been true....that the bow should have been able to cast an arrow farther from the same brace height.

Switching to aluminum shafts solved about half the problem; lowering the brace height solved the remainder. I can't say whether your bow's tune would be similarly affected at higher altitudes, but this certainly is something you need to be aware of and prepare for if you head into the mountains.

There doesn't seem to be any way to prevent the bow's changing. I've been back to Colorado and hunted in the 10,000-plus elevation twice since then. I'd do some basic tuning at home, then wait to finish the job when I arrived in Colorado. Both times I needed to adjust the brace height, and both times the bow and I shot fine once I did that.

Chapter 5
Bowhunting

What follows, in no particular order, are various aspects of hunting which are good to know, plus a couple of hunting stories. I'm assuming you're past the beginner stages of bowhunting and are somewhere in the intermediate stage or above that. You may or may not be practicing some of the things I'll talk about, but whether or not you are, I thought they were important enough to include. Hope they help your hunting and give you some interesting reading.

TIDAL CHARTS & MOON PHASES
We've all had days in the woods where nothing, absolutely nothing, is happening. There are no birds singing, no squirrels feeding. It's totally dead ... and then all of a sudden everything comes to life. We start seeing birds fluttering around, squirrels coming down trees, everything feeding. If you'll take note when that happens, the moon is either in the major or minor phase, probably the major.

Obviously there are circumstances which would override or otherwise heavily influence the feeding times. Hunter pressure is one. An approaching storm front is another. These are best described as "local" conditions.

The moon affects hunting success, but not in the way we usually believe (full moon -- deer feed all night -- lousy hunting). Since I do most of my whitetail hunting within 300 miles of the ocean, I also pay attention to tidal charts. Tides are governed by the moon's position. Use this moon information to select when you should hunt.

The best hunting is when the moon is up about an hour high above the horizon when the sun goes down in the afternoon. I see considerable animal movement at that time. That would be equated to a tidal change.

If you hunt within about 300 miles of a body of water large enough to have tides, get the tidal charts for the numbers of days you will be hunting. The high tide - low tide is the same as the major feed - minor feed.

When you can see the moon earlier in the day, then the hunting and fishing is better. When the moon is coming up it is a major feed; when the moon is going down it is a minor feed. Actually, this particular year I've paid a lot of attention to the position of the moon. Any time the moon was up above the horizon I was on stand, because when the moon is visible above the horizon, that's the best time to hunt.

Second best time is when the moon is rising on the opposite side of the earth. During a full moon on the opposite side of the earth, there will be minor feeds at sunrise and sunset and a major feed in the middle of the day.

Brad Smith, a friend from Tennessee, and I were hunting in south Alabama a couple of years ago. Brad had shot a deer the afternoon before, and the evidence on the shaft and on the ground indicated a shot through the intestines. So we didn't track it at all that night. The weather forecast was good -- cool and clear.

We went out at daylight the next morning to track the animal. We found the animal after a couple of hours, dressed it out and loaded it up. We were coming out on our ATVs about 10:45 a.m. when I noticed the moon was up about an hour high above the horizon.

I told Brad, "I'll see you. I'm going to my stand."

He took his animal back to camp and I went on stand. Fifteen minutes later I had another deer on the ground. That deer was feeding on acorns, just moseying along.

I've shot deer the same way at 1:00 in the afternoon.

Relative to moon rise and set, here are the things to remember:
* The NEW MOON rises at sunrise and sets at sunset;
* The FULL MOON rises at sunset and sets at sunrise;
* The FIRST QUARTER MOON rises at noon and sets at midnight;
* The LAST QUARTER MOON rises at midnight and sets at noon.

The best possible time of the month to hunt is on a new moon, because it will have three feeding periods during daylight hours:

1) A major feed occurs one hour before to one hour after the moon is directly overhead. This occurs any time the moon is directly overhead, no matter which time of the month.

2) A minor feed occurs 30 minutes before to 30 minutes after moonrise.

3) A minor feed occurs 30 minutes before to 30 minutes after moonset. The full moon is poor hunting because it has only two minor feeds corresponding with the usual times deer feed and there is no major feeding period during daylight hours.

The rut DOES NOT make all these conditions null and void, because does aren't as affected. Bucks are looking for hot does over a long period of time, whereas does are looking for bucks only during the peak of their estrus. The remainder of the rut, the does are pretty much in their usual feeding and movement patterns, except for when a buck is harassing them to see if they are ready.

Paying attention to the moon phases last fall gave me one of the best, yet one of the most frustrating, whitetail hunts I've ever had. I saw four Pope and Young-class bucks in one day but couldn't get a shot at any of them. Made me a nervous wreck.

I selected dates to hunt by using the lunar chart, aiming to pick a time with as many feeding periods during daylight hours as possible. The next-to-last week of January looked to be my best chance. At that time, the rut would be going strong in the area I planned to hunt. I knew large bucks lived in the area; during my scouting I'd seen several huge rubs and scrapes. I arrived at deer camp one day early to hang stands in areas I'd already scouted.

The first morning was spent on the "swamp stand", an area with a pine plantation at the base of the hill where the swamp begins. The plantation abruptly ends into a stand of mature hardwoods, which is a feeding area for deer. Approximately half a mile from here is a large pasture and green fields where deer feed at night.

Nothing showed the first two hours that morning. Then I sensed more than heard something moving behind me. I turned my head slowly to the left, and after some eyeballing finally spotted a deer's legs in the pine plantation. I watched it half a minute or so before the deer moved out to where I could see it fully....a humongous buck. P&Y #1 of the day. He stood there a bit but didn't move close enough for a shot. Then he actually walked out the logging trail I had walked in on and out of sight. I tried grunting and rattling. No response. The buck had come out of the low ground. It wasn't trailing a doe, just travelling. His antlers would score, in my estimation, 140-145.

I saw several does and small bucks moving across the ridge above me after this. An hour or so later, I saw a doe coming straight to me from my left, from east to west. I stood and got in shooting position, in case a buck followed her. Sure enough, P&Y #2 came

● *Ferguson with a fat six-pointer taken in southern Alabama.*

into sight, a good eight-pointer, scoring in the 130s. The doe came to a big scrape not more than 10 paces from my tree stand and urinated in that scrape. The buck came in behind her and paused. He needed to take three more steps for me to get a shot.

The buck grunted one time, real soft, sounding almost like a cat purring. That doe was not ready. She bolted and ran into the pine plantation. The buck, rather than coming to the scrape where I could shoot, cut the corner to head her off. The buck chased that doe in the plantation probably five minutes, only 30 yards from me, but in cover so thick there was no shot. Then they moved out of sight, still in the plantation.

I remained on stand until lunch, thinking I'd already had more than a full day's hunting excitement. At lunch my host, Billy Perryman, suggested I hunt a hill area nearby. I looked the area over and hung a stand on a trail leading uphill to a green field on top of the hill.

I began seeing deer within 30 seconds after I got on stand, coming from the hollow, up the drainage, under my stand and up to the green patch . I lost count of the spikes, button bucks, small racks and does. **At two o'clock in the afternoon, the moon was almost directly overhead.**

Near sundown, I glanced across the field, and saw the P&Y #3 of the day, 400-500 yards off, chasing a doe. I could see good antler mass and spread. This tended to frustrate me somewhat.

The next deer that came by me was a doe, which I fully intended to shoot. But I had made the mistake of putting my stand in a too-small pine tree. When I stood up, she caught the movement of the pine. The deer didn't bolt but made a wide circle around me and went on to the field. I remained standing, because there was only one hour to sundown.

The next deer past was a six-pointer. Billy had already told me that bucks in this area often have only six points, no brow tines. He told me to take out such deer as culls. So I shot that buck.

Waiting for the necessary time to pass, and waiting for dark, I heard a deer coming from directly behind me. I turned to see what it was. Turned out to be a buck with the widest antler spread I've ever seen on a whitetail. I bet it was close to 30 inches, or maybe an actual 30 inches. The beams were so wide they looked out of place. Just humongous.

For some dumb reason, reflex action mostly, I stood up and moved too fast doing so. I couldn't shoot, because I'd already taken my one deer for the day. (Alabama law is one deer a day during bow season.) This deer also saw the tree shake and bolted. This was P&Y #4 in the same day.

I hunted the swamp on the remaining mornings of the four-day trip. In the afternoons I hunted green patches where does congregate. I saw small bucks and plenty of does. In swamp every morning, I would see a deer walking east to west where the pine plantation met mature hardwood. He had a spike on his left side, nothing on the right. Looked like he never had had anything on the right, because there was no antler-base scar, just hair.

On the fourth day, I pulled my stand and told Billy about the one-spiked deer and how he should take his son out there and let his son shoot the deer. Billy suggested I shoot the deer. I explained how I had to leave to get ready for a show, and he explained to me that I'd lose only a couple hours of sleep and I should go shoot it.

I was there before daylight and hung the stand. Since I was running a little late, instead of getting my normal eight steps high (12-14 feet), I put only six tree steps in. After being on stand about 30 minutes, I saw a deer coming and figured it was the one-spike. I stood up and folded my seat back, concerned more about how to get the deer out and still be able to leave on time than on watching the deer.

When the deer walked out, I could see it was a doe. Relief. I'm not shooting it. So I watched it for three minutes, then saw a larger deer coming behind her. I figured this one would be the spike. It walked 30 steps to the south of first doe, stepped out and proved to be a big doe -- roughly 120 pounds, which for Alabama is a big doe.

I watched them feed five minutes, then noticed the first doe had its head up, ears forward, staring past me. It stood motionless more than a minute. I turned my head slowly to look behind me, and there stood the monster buck, eight steps behind me. I almost fell OUT of the tree. This was the P&Y #1 buck I had seen four days earlier. His antlers looked three inches in diameter at their bases, so massive the main beams looked cupped. The ends of the tines were blunted like your thumb.

I was going to be Mr. Cool, so I turned around and e-e-e-ased the bow up onto my boot toe. I had convinced myself the buck would walk to the first doe and pass my tree at five steps. I waited and waited. He didn't show.

I couldn't stand it any more. When I turned to look, the buck had already walked behind a brush screen toward the second doe. No shot. Fifteen steps, but no shot.

The buck walked to the second doe. She urinated, which didn't help my cause at all, then turned and started to walk away. Naturally, the buck followed. If she stayed on this path, she would cross 15-18 steps in front of me, with the buck right behind her and very shootable.

The doe walked to the edge of the clearing, hopped over a blown-down sapling stubbed about three feet off the ground, and cut through the edge of the clearing. The buck was 20 yards behind her. He came to the sapling. I had the bow 3/4 drawn. But instead of hopping the blow-down, the buck ducked and went under it, and the limbs and brush in front of me screened him. No shot. He turned and went out the edge of the clearing. No shot there either.

I had what you would normally call a screaming, running, stomping, cussing fit.

I stayed until lunch and saw one more buck. Took my stand out at lunch and went home.

Those bucks are all still there.

I will return.

If my stand had been at its normal height I could have shot over the branches that screened the buck. That really upset me. Also, playing the part of Mr. Cool didn't help me, either. I told myself all the way home that was the luckiest deer in the world, because I felt I hadn't screwed up anywhere else, other than setting my stand too low. But I had. I took my eye off him. I was not in a strain. I could have leaned against the tree and continued to watch, and then when I would have seen him turn and go to the second doe instead of the first one, it would have been a 10 step, easy shot. He was in the open.

I can't wait to get back down there this year. Ol' Lucky definitely is a shootable deer; I saw him too many times. He is patternable. He gave me every opportunity. I was so intent on not messing up that I messed up.

There was no trail. He just came out of the brush. Billy told me that deer has been there at least four years. He rubs trees at least eight inches in diameter. I have no idea how many points he has; the massiveness was too awesome. Those deer have food, cover and practically no hunting pressure -- and good genetics. Some of those deer are Wisconsin deer...they are descendants of transplants from Wisconsin. The 120-pound doe looked like a yearling standing next to this buck.

I get excited again just talking about it. That was NOT your typical Alabama buck.

BEST BUCK SIGHTINGS

I've always had more success with deer in general in the afternoons. I see more animals and they seem to be calmer, more susceptible to letting you move on them and get a shot. It's not because I hunt more in the afternoons; I hunt mornings and afternoons fairly equally. It seems to run counter to what you might think, but I'm just relating my personal experiences with animals in general, particularly the white-tail deer. I think deer relax during their mid-day bedding, and their metabolism most likely slows down. Hunters probably have been out of the woods since around 9 a.m., and if it's a warm day, those deer are going to be as relaxed as they're ever going to get.

When hunters are in the woods all day, then those same deer will be jittery in the afternoon. So a lot depends upon hunting pressure.

But I would also like to say that I have had better success on buck deer in the mornings than the afternoons. Most of the morning buck action has been shortly after daylight. The deer were either feeding or travelling. The ones I've had the best success with and taken the most of would be bucks that were travelling toward their daytime hide-outs and picking food along the way. Just moseying through and heading back.

In trophy management areas I hunted last year, I never saw trophy bucks in the afternoon, not even near bedding areas, except for one buster just at dark. Big bucks are more nocturnal. The next day I set up 100 yards down that big buck's trail back into the woods. About 15 minutes before dark, a forky passed and I could hear another deer walking behind it but not too close. That second deer got to within 30 yards of me, stopped in a thicket and never moved. At last light, the big deer was still standing in the thicket or had slipped out silently without my catching any movement. At any rate, when I

● *When conditions are right, and you expect to see deer, stalk the stand. Hunt your way to it. Sometimes there really will be a deer feeding near it. After all, that's why you put the stand there to begin with, isn't it?*

decided to leave I slipped down quietly to be able to hear it if it moved off, but there wasn't a sound. This was before the rut. I think the big deer was using the little buck as a scout.

My morning success with bucks has been largely governed by whether or not the moon was up, but in general I see more bucks in the morning than on afternoon hunts.

In all my hunting, I hunt bottlenecks between the obvious feeding areas and bedding areas....their daytime hideouts. In the morning I set up closer to their daytime bedding areas; in the afternoon I tend to hunt closer to the major food sources than I do in the transition areas. I'm still hunting the bottlenecks, but that would lead to seeing more young deer, does and small bucks, in the afternoon.

I know hunters who have had excellent success hunting terrain features only. They pay little or no attention to food sources. Hunting saddles, for instance. Ridges, too. You can locate those on a topo map and position yourself well. These are forms of bottlenecks.

I also know hunters who pay no attention to terrain features and hunt food sources. The theory being that those deer are going to eat something, so find what they're eating and be in an appropriate location when they come to eat.

I kind of blend the two together, because I believe it increases my chances for success almost geometrically. So any time I can find the appropriate terrain features fairly near food, that's the place to be.

When the terrain changes, that becomes a transition zone. There are lots of things helping deer move and hide in such conditions.

The inside corners of edges are another form of bottleneck which can be excellent places to set up. By "edges", I mean the edges of woods bordering an open feeding area.

Inside corners are good afternoon stand sites. Locate the feeder trails and the perimeter trail. Set up further into the woods behind the perimeter trail, watching as many feeder trails as you can. That perimeter trail will be 10 to 20 paces back into the woods, so I'm generally set up 30 to 40 paces back in the woods. This places me behind the perimeter trail. An inside corner simply will be more likely to have more than one feeder trail and is thus a wonderful bottleneck to hunt. If there are terrain changes nearby, or as an integral part of the inside corner, expect to find even more feeder trails.

The best time to hunt such an area depends upon your approach route. If your approach will be through a grassy field, the afternoon will most likely be better, simply because the deer will have bedded further back in the woods. This is generally the same with agricultural crops, except those such as corn which are tall enough to provide excellent cover. In such cases, hunting the edge of the field and of the woods may place you slap in the middle of the action, with deer moving in both directions.

When an open field is just a weed field, tall weeds make excellent deer bedding area, so your approach should be down the edge of the field instead of through the field. You'll also want to set up closer to the edge of the field so you can see into the tall weeds and back into the woods. When the open field is pasture grass, walk through the open field and set up back further in the woods.

Watch the wind, watch the wind, watch the wind. If one spot isn't right, go to another one. This is the value of having several good stand sites ready.

ON STAND BEFORE DAYLIGHT?

I move into an area in the early half-light; I don't move into an area before daylight. I prefer to wait until there's enough light to let me see how to get to my stand without the use of a flashlight. I move much more quietly when I can see the brush and twigs in my path, when I can see where I'm going to place my feet. The woods looks different in full darkness. An area we see as semi-open in daylight hours may look thick under the glare of just a flashlight beam. Thicker cover may look like an impenetrable jungle in a flashlight's path. The terrain and the cover are unrecognizable, which can lead to a lot of extra stumbling around and brush cracking when we get lost...well, maybe not lost, but a little bit off course. There's an additional reason to go in when you can see well: A lot of times, particularly if the minor or major feed happens to take place just before daylight, may be animals still feeding within good shot range of your stand when you get there. If you wait until there's enough light available, you stand a chance of getting a shot at an animal on your way to your stand.

Under those conditions, the best way to describe my approach would be to say that I **stalk the stand**. I come in from downwind and stalk the stand. To do it properly, I have to convince myself there IS an animal under my stand and make a stalking approach as if there was. Every once in a while an animal is there. That can get kind of exciting.

Sometimes it will take me an hour to move the last 100 yards to my stand. Again, this depends on the minor and major feeding periods that are predicted. At other times, if the moon is coming up or going down at 10:00 a.m., I'm in no particular hurry to get on stand. I'll hit the woods at half-light, mosey on in there and eventually get to the stand somewhere between 8:30 and 9:00.

When the moon is slated to be coming up, correlating with the sunrise, then I'll hurry to my stand. I then want to be on stand between daylight and the time the sun actually rises.

During the rut, everything goes out the window, except for one thing -- that's when I hunt does, because bucks are hunting does, too, at that time. So if I've got a green field that the does particularly like, or an oak tree that the does particularly like, I'll be there. I've had reasonably good success with this, but keep in mind that I'm not a trophy hunter. I have, however, taken my share of bucks, some of theme fairly decent bucks.

BIGGER BUCKS

I like to hunt deer, I like to eat deer. But if I'm after a particular buck and I have found his scrapes and rub lines, and maybe seen him hanging around a particular oak flat, then you can bet I'll look for a particular tree in that oak flat that deer seem to prefer. I'll set my stand to cover as many approaches to that food tree as practical.

Getting into your stand quickly in the morning so you can let the area "cool down" shouldn't always be the main concern. I don't believe you can fool a deer's nose. They have a super sense of smell. I've tried various things. The best thing to do is to approach a stand from an area the deer tend not to use, if at all possible. Stay off the deer trails. You're going to be noisier moving through cover where there is no trail, and you're going to be making noises where deer aren't accustomed to hearing noises, but you can and you must hold it to a minimum. If you approach right, the alarm bells your approach noise send to deer in the area will be minimal. That's another reason I prefer to wait until daylight.

If you do it right, the negatives are not even close to all the positives gained by doing so. Bowhunting is a game of playing the odds. The odds are that if you cross a trail, the deer is going to smell you. So stay off the trail. Even if you make a little more noise, even if you're going to leave a little human scent on the tall grass or on the shrubbery or the brush going it....you just have to play the odds. Do everything you can to give the deer the least chance to detect your presence, and at the same time maneuver yourself into the best position for seeing deer and getting a good shot at an unalarmed animal.

Negatives:

1) Noises you make. Let's call them sounds instead of noises. Sounds are natural. Noises are sounds that are out of place and/or unnatural. If you cannot be silent, make sounds instead of noises. There are all sorts of natural sounds in the woods, but the natural sound of human movement is rhythmic, and that's bad. There isn't any other rhythmic sound in the woods even remotely like the sound of a walking human.

2) Human odor. Yes, it's quieter to move on a trail, and we'll probably lay down more scent when we move through brush and weeds off a trail, but I certainly would rather have more scent there and none on the trail. I don't mean to make this sound like you should thrash your way through the puckerbrush just to stay off a deer trail. Pick your spots.

I have on occasion cut a light trail through a thick area, using a hand clippers. This leaves less of my scent and makes my next approach through there, however later that may be, a little quieter. The neat thing about this is that if you hunt this same area again next year, you will find deer will be using that trail you cut for them through the thick growth.

A good bit of a careful approach is best handled by careful preparation -- keeping yourself and your gear clean and non-odorous. I just try NOT to smell like a human. I want to disappear, scent-wise and sight-wise. That's another value to taking it easy on your way into your stand. The faster you move, the more you work up a sweat, the quicker you begin manufacturing alarming human odor. Playing it slow and cool has several advantages.

I've read you should wear rubber boots or rubber bottom boots, but I've had limited success with that. On occasion, I've had animals walk across where I had walked, without smelling I had been there. I've also had animals turn inside out when they walked where I walked. No matter what footwear you use, keep foreign odors off them and their soles. Wear them only in the woods, changing at your vehicle and storing them in a plastic bag. This is another detail, but the road to success is paved with little details carefully attended to.

One thing you can do, if you have your pants cuffs outside your boots, is to stuff the cuffs inside your boot tops. This will stop air flow down the inside of your pants leg and thus reduce the amount of scent you leave. You'll also conserve body heat, which makes this a good thing in colder weather.

I use some of the commercial scent eliminators, but mostly I was myself with unscented soap and a good wash cloth, and I wash my hunting clothes with unscented deodorant then hang them outside to dry. When they're dry, I put them in a plastic bag with some leaves and branches and dirt from the area I'll be hunting. Anything to NOT smell like a human.

I use a few cover scents, too, but I do it carefully. It wouldn't make sense to use cover scents of animals that aren't around here much, if at all. Haven't smelled a skunk around here in years. Besides, they only spray when alarmed.

I know that doe deer, especially doe deer with small fawns, tend to come unglued when they cross bobcat tracks or bobcat scent. No way would I use bobcat as a cover scent. I've not had any luck with fox cover scent. I did see a deer in Virginia stop when it came to a fox's tracks and go no farther. It would not cross where the fox had walked. I tried raccoon scent a few times, with mixed results.

I have, however, been pleased with cedar oil masking scent. I hunt several areas with heavy cedar cover, so it's a natural there. I liberally doused it on my clothes, boots, gloves, stand, the leather wrap on my bow handle -- anything that could touch brush or absorb my scent. Many times deer walked close to where I had been, with no sign they scented me. Vegetative scent is a natural. You need to pick your spots, I believe, matching the scent to the native local vegetation.

In some swampy south Alabama areas, the cedar scent didn't work as well. I had better apparent luck there with a scent neutralizer. I practically poured it on myself, because I believe that when you're using a scent-neutralizing agent, use it like you owned the company that made it.

I wear an unscented deodorant (Mitchum's brand name). The chemicals in the deodorant close up your pores, so that's a plus. And with no sweet scent to make you smell pretty, that's another plus.

I use no commercial scents for lures. The best lure in the woods is the sound of acorns falling. If that doesn't work, the sound of grass growing will.

Once the acorns are gone .... find the alternative food source. They've got to eat. Here in the South, once the acorns are gone the deer will be on the green briar and honeysuckle.

TREE STAND PLACEMENT

There's been a lot written about tree stand hunting and tree stand placement, but one thing that is constantly overlooked and is probably just as important as the placement of the stand is the **positioning of the stand on the tree**. I've hunted from numerous stands that were in a good place, in the right tree, but the stands were out of position in the tree. Sometimes it's something as simple as a right-hand shooter setting up a treestand, then a left-hand shooter attempting to use it. Or vice versa. Try that sometime; there just isn't any way.

When you're setting up your tree stand, scope out the area around the tree thoroughly. This is especially important when you're hunting a couple or more trails, and/or when you're in an area the first couple of times. In a new area, you never can be sure which direction the deer will come from. This can be even more critical during the rut, because bucks are all over the place as they check trails and scrapes, and as they sniff out the ready does.

You sometimes can improve a stand's position immensely simply by changing the angle 15 degrees. A lot of times this can increase your field of shooting 30 to 45 degrees, sometimes much more than that if the tree is such that you can lean out around it and shoot behind you. The best rule of thumb is to position yourself so you can cover the most area without needing to stand up. Obviously, you'll stand at times just to stretch your muscles and to give yourself the widest range of flexibility (turning at the ankles, knees, hips, waist and shoulders) for best coverage, but the seated-on-the-stand test is a good place to begin. Too many bowhunters position their stand so it faces the middle of the area they want to cover. This is self-limiting. The stand out to be positioned more to the right for a right hand shooter and more to the left for a left-hand shooter. This will enable you to turn your body further to the left for a right-hand shooter and further to the right for a left-hand shooter.

Where you have multiple trees, multiple food sources, try to position the stand where you can see and shoot to several different places, rather than singling out what may seem to be the best one.

Some bowhunters feel they remain more calm by positioning their stand on the side of the tree opposite the direction from which they expect deer to approach. This way, they won't be tempted to watch the deer as it approaches, and the tree trunk will do a better job of hiding their small movements. This scares me. I've had too many deer smell where I've gone up the tree, even with some of the cover scents and scent eliminators. I still like to see them approaching.

Under what circumstances have they smelled where I climbed the tree? Cool, damp days. They were right under me. The argument

● You'll probably have better results (fewer spooked deer) if you put your tree stand ABOVE the lowest limb. Deer seem to look up to the lowest limb for danger, dismissing anything above that level.

● Left photos: A pocket on the underside of your tree stand holds a chain, keeping it from clanking. The nylon loop on a webbed belt is secure and quick, letting you set your tree stand swiftly, quietly and with minimal physical contact with the tree, so you'll leave less human odor. With a ladder stand that sets in place in a hurry, and a safety pull-up rope, you can be in place and waiting quickly, quietly and with little human scent dispersal. No sweat, in other words.

could be made that I was set up too close to where they were approaching, that I should have been further away so they couldn't scent me. A couple of times that would have been true, however, in most cases I had no choice. It was either the tree I was in or the food tree, and the only time to be in a food tree is when there is no other tree available....and for it to work, you'd better be on your very best behavior up there in that food tree. Deer approaching right at you have too many eyes, and a deer right under you is a poor shot angle. When that happens to me, I tell my hunting partners the deer weren't supposed to approach from where they did anyway. They were just dumb deer, and probably lost, too.

For years I used climbing stands almost exclusively, because climbing into trees is quick, easy and fairly quiet. Then Jerry Simmons told me he had found it productive to set his stand ABOVE at least the first limb, because deer tend to look up to the first limb but no higher (unless you give them a reason, obviously). That has proven to be true 100 percent of the time. So now, whenever possible, I strap a fixed-position portable onto the tree trunk ABOVE the first limb, and there I wait. Deer seem to scan the tree up to that first limb, then turn their attention elsewhere if not alarmed. If they catch movement, that's a different story, of course.

Fixed position stands are easier to put in place and generally offer quieter access once the stand is in position. And, of course, setting up above the first limb , you can't climb to it with a climber anyway. You could use a climbing model to hang in position, but it would be used, obviously, as a non-climber. A fixed position stand generally is more versatile -- it can be put on larger or smaller trees, and in trees that would be too much work to get into with a climbing treestand.

I have had no problems shooting a longbow from any stand that any other bow could be used from, with one exception. I love to hunt from double-trunk or three-trunk trees because they hide you much better and motion is more obscured. I also shoot with my bow canted. When I'm setting up in a double trunk or three-trunk tree, I have to be careful about the positioning of my stand to make sure I can draw with my bow canted.

To minimize leaving my scent, I don't go in and set up a stand and come out and go back and get on stand. When I find an area scouting that I want to hunt, on the day I decide to hunt it, I'll go in an hour and a half to two hours earlier than I'd normally go in, set up my stand and stay there.

Generally speaking, your first time in an area is your best chance at numbers of deer or quality of deer. Because every time you go back into this area, no matter how careful you are, you're going to

● *Belt-on camo pouch holds all the tools Ferguson needs to get up a tree and put up an instant stand — woodpecker drill, slip-in spikes, and strong nylon rope to clip around the tree so your hands are free.*

● *Spring bear hunting....carp shooting....a wild hog hunt. Three great ways to make your bowhunting a several-seasons sport.*

leave scent and give deer more opportunities to see, hear or smell you. Either while you're there or at any other time of day or night. You can't avoid leaving some amount of scent.

That's why I always have in my pack my drill and my steps. When I'm scouting, if I see an area I like I can set up instantly, or drill it and peg it so when I come back later with my stand I can get in and hang the stand quickly and quietly.

To further minimize leaving my scent, I hang my gear about head high above the ground on a pull-up cord while installing climbing steps and placing the tree stand. I wear cotton gloves. I think other gloves can carry just as much scent. Besides, I'm careful what I touch and don't touch on the way in to my stand, careful what I touch and don't touch at my stand site. Basically, I try to be a non-presence.

Besides, I do not cut shooting lanes; I pick natural holes to shoot through. This further helps keep my movement at the stand site to a minimum. Clearing shooting lanes is a lot of extra movement and leaves a lot of human scent, in addition to altering the immediate landscape. You move around, you grasp vegetation, you may work up a sweat, you move to get rid of the cut brush and branches, etc. It's too much.

One day last year I broke my own rule on that. I had seen deer the previous afternoon traveling down a shallow ditch. I put up my stand so I could shoot into the ditch, but covering brush on the side of the ditch was too thick, and I couldn't shoot over it. I got down there with my hand clippers and my folding saw and knocked down enough greenery to open a couple of shooting lanes. I saw deer alright, but they would come to the first bush I'd cut, smell where I'd been, and away they'd go, back where they came from. They knew it was safe back there.

To check for natural shooting openings, focus your binoculars on the deer trail(s) you're watching, then move the focus back from the trail toward yourself to see whether there are any limbs and twigs in the way of the arrow's visualized flight path. This obviously also then becomes good practice for visualizing **and learning** the arrow's flight path. Do this as soon as you get on stand, not when the animal is walking down the trail toward you.

FUNNELING DEER

Jerry Simmons has done it successfully. He uses his undershirt or jacket, some article of clothing, positioned on a deer trail. This is necessary when you're hunting two trails close together but can't decide which to hunt, or when they both can't be covered from one stand. He blocks one trail and watches the other trail. Other bowhunters do this, too, I know.

Some hunters use inflated balloons tied on bushes in such a manner that as deer shy away from them they drift into a pattern -- right past the hunter's stand.

If you want a more-permanent block, pile some logs and brush across a trail and then clip a new trail around it where you want it to go. Deer prefer to follow the line of least resistance, as long as they can stay covered or, if exposed, be exposed for just a very short time.

THE MOMENT OF TRUTH

Knowing what to do and when to do it as the deer first comes into view and then moves within good shot range is a learned art. You can help yourself a great deal by watching deer in the off-season, and by watching big game animals in a zoo, studying how they move, what they do before they move and as they move, their body postures, body language in head, ears, tail, etc. But nothing beats being able to say: "Been there. Done that."

You start getting ready as soon as you see the deer. Move in slow motion. If you're seated, stand up and get ready to shoot. This includes raising your bow arm and getting the bow turned in the position you want it. You're ready to draw and shoot. Reason for that -- even though you maybe aren't planning to shoot this particular animal, if you let this animal get in and then the buck comes in that you want to shoot, you've got twice the number of eyes, twice the ears and noses to get past.

I do NOT watch their head, I can tell you that. I look at their feet, I look at their tail. I look at anything except the head. I don't want to make eye contact; that's the quickest way to spook a deer.

I have had deer see me, and I have closed my eyes and refused to look at them, only to listen to where the deer were. I remained motionless. And when I heard them start walking again, opened my eyes. I've been able to take most of those animals.

What did they see? They saw a roundish box sitting up on the side of the tree, and they didn't know exactly what it was. Maybe they thought I was the world's largest squirrel. On the other hand....

A couple of years ago, two does came in to my stand. My bow was hanging on a limb next to me. They caught me out of position, totally flat-footed. I didn't move....had my eyes closed....but the lead doe saw something she didn't like. I listened and heard them start moving. When I looked out through the slit in my eyelids, the second deer was moving, feeding, but the lead doe was still looking up at me. She kept me pinned down for maybe four minutes, until she started feeding. I got the bow, stood up, got ready to shoot

-- they were behind the food tree from me -- and that lead doe came out from behind the tree, looked up at me and saw that whatever it was had moved. She was outta there. No head bobbing, no foot stomping, no nothing but blast off.

I also know that deer leave some type of alarm scent that is distinguishable to other deer. I've seen it so many times....a deer is spooked and runs off into the wind, so it's upwind of you. A while later, a different deer comes to that trail upwind of you and stops, then bolts. It didn't smell you. You weren't moving, and it didn't see you.

HUNTING FROM THE GROUND

I don't hunt from the ground much. Many of the places I hunt near home are so thick that you can't effectively hunt them from anywhere other than a treestand. However, later in the season, it isn't too bad. The deer are more exposed because leaves have fallen and you can see farther in the woods. There's less food available, so they are moving more. They also move more randomly than earlier in the year because they can't concentrate on the staple food sources like acorn and various crop fields. And since the leaves have been down a while, they're going to be damp and quieter to walk on than when they first fell.

If at all possible, you want the sun at your back; you want to be able to go into the wind or into a good crosswind, and you want to take advantage of the cover just like the animals take advantage of it. It's all slow motion stuff, slipping from bush to bush or tree to tree, staying on the shaded side. Hustling across the open areas to minimize your exposure....just like deer generally do.

The best possible scenario for me is to see an animal a couple of hundred yards ahead and watch it a while. I want to determine its general feeding direction and then circle so I can get in front of it and ambush it. Doesn't work that way very often, but it sure is fun trying.

The last animal I shot while I was on the ground like that was a nice doe. I had moved into position, but the doe, when I looked back, was still where I had first seen it. I had passed it by 200 yards. So now that the wind was in my favor, I began a slower-than-usual stalk on it. The sun was at my back, too. I got to within 35 steps before running out of cover. So I just stayed put, leaned up beside a tree. The deer eventually fed toward me. As I made ready for the shot, in my peripheral vision I noted movement off to my left. I turned my head to look and there were three deer I hadn't seen before. The wind was right, so they fed in totally unaware of my presence. I shot one of those deer, because they were closer, unalarmed and the same size as the first doe.

Footwear for this type of hunting needs to have reasonably soft-soled boots so you can feel the sticks under your feet and avoid them before putting your weight down. It's a comfort to have water resistant footwear, too, because morning dew on grass, weeds and brush can give you a soaking as you move through it.

● Higher camera angle, top photo, shows Ferguson clearly. Bottom photo, from much lower angle — the deer's eye level — has Ferguson well camouflaged. The idea is to peek over the bank and be high enough so your arrow will just clear.

● A wade-able creek can be a hunting hotspot, year after year. Food supply is good: thermal currents should be in your favor at almost all times; you can move quietly and remain hidden, and deer don't look for danger from the middle of a creek bed. Any movement they see will be down at small-game level, and thus unalarming.

HUNTING A CREEK

If you hunt an area where there's a hard-bottom, shallow creek, that's a super place to hunt and a super place to stalk. Knee boots or hip boots are required, and if you're real lucky, you will have dry feet. But you can move very quietly, and you've got the banks of the creek as cover. Just slip along -- right up the creek -- peeking up over the bank occasionally. I've taken a lot of deer like that. Plus, your scent is going to stay in the creek and run down slope, unless there's one hell of an unusual thermal.

First of all, the hunting I'm talking about is early October through the end of January 31. That's the Alabama season. The white-tail deer rut doesn't happen until mid-January in my part of the country. Again, most of my still hunting takes place later in the year because there's less food available and animals seem to be moving more randomly to find food. At that time of year, there is more food down along the creek bed. The water oak acorns will be falling all year, but especially that time of year. There's also green briar and honeysuckle down along the creek. So creek hunting that time of year has a lot going for it. You can move quietly, the scent is controlled, you can move without being seen, and you're moving through an area with a high concentration of food available for the deer. Besides that, the snakes aren't as bad then....

One of the first deer I killed along a creek, I was actually sitting on the bank of the creek with my feet dangling over. It was a warm day, but it was probably in December or early January. I saw a nice six-point buck about 50 yards from me, standing ankle deep in the creek, drinking. Then he hopped up on the bank. I waited, hoping he would feed down in front of me on the opposite side of the creek.

When he didn't show up after about one hour, I got down in the creek and very slowly, without picking my feet clear of the water, just shuffling along, got to the point where the deer was when I saw him in the creek earlier. I peeked up over the steep bank with just my eyes over the top, and there he was about 15 steps from the creek, still standing there, feeding on honeysuckle. He didn't go far.

The next year, the creek became one of my favorite places to hunt, and I never hunted from a tree in that creek bottom.

One morning I went to the same place where I had been sitting the year before when I first saw that six-pointer. I was standing there, leaning against a tree, when a doe and a four-point buck walked out on the opposite side of the creek from me. They were relaxed, feeding and moseying, with no idea I was anywhere near. They never saw my draw. I got the four-pointer.

The next day I went back to the same place and got a spike

bucks. It was standing almost in the same tracks as the four-pointer.

Then one morning I went to the same creek, but probably 100 yards deeper in the woods, because the food source where I had been hunting had been pretty much depleted. The deer seemed to be moving deeper into the swamp area. I was sitting on a log .... deer started running past me, and it not only was a good feeding are, but it turned out to be a bottleneck. There were some guys down the creek from me who were ready to make a deer drive with dogs, and I had all the deer coming past me. I saw 23 deer in less than 15 minutes.

When you're down in the creek, peeking over the top, any motion the deer sees is going to appear to be at a level where it's accustomed to seeing small movement .... close to the ground, and thus unalarming. Secondly, you've got a great angle on a deer's vital areas. From that low position, your arrow should get both lungs, and it won't have much bone to go through. It's as perfect a shot as you're going to get. And if there's water running, it will cover the small sounds you may make. If the water isn't running enough, just slush your feet in the water without splashing alarmingly. If you have to make noise, don't be rhythmic.

DEER BODY LANGUAGE

Once a deer becomes alarmed, maybe has even spotted you, you know it's got you nailed, so watch it carefully. It will look one way, it will look another way, and it's going to run. It will always look two directions. So while it's looking in the first direction, if you're going to shoot, you'd better be shooting in a hurry. Once it looks the second direction, it's going to run in one of those two directions. You have the opportunity while the animal is looking away to draw the bow.

Tail twitch -- that's an all-clear signal after they've looked around a while and didn't see anything to become alarmed over.

I don't look at the eyes, but I'm vaguely aware of the head position, what they're doing in relation to the ears moving, jerky steps of a deer when it's really tense.

If the deer hears something it's not sure exactly where it came from, rather than turning the head in all directions and looking, it tends to move just the ears, swiveling them around, trying to locate the source of the sound. That's less of them to move, less to be seen, and they can check one or two directions with their ears and cover still more ground with their eyes.

A deer that is ready to explode out of an area has much more animated movement. Their actions are real jerky. Best thing there is to pass the shot.

Body language AFTER THE SHOT is just as important. A lot of

times it will tell you where the animal is hit or how hard it has been hit. Everyone knows about the gut shot, with the deer acting instantly sick and often humping up.

When shot through the heart, a deer tends to grunt on arrow impact. It takes off and will be running full speed. The tail will be flagging; it won't be tucked down. The tail will be sticking straight out and for some reason it tends to corkscrew, just before it collapses. So if you see a big swirl of white flag, expect to find that deer near there, but not necessarily straight ahead. Sometimes deer turn off as they fall and you can walk right past them if you're moving too fast or not looking close enough.

A deer's eyes are on the sides of its head. A deer looking 90 degrees away from you can still see you draw. That's all the more reason to know when to finish the draw and when to shoot. I get into position early, when I first see the deer approaching. And if this is a deer I want to shoot, there's no problem holding my bow up. My longbow has a mass weight of less than one pound. With the adrenaline pumping, I think I could hold the bow with an extended bow arm indefinitely at the ready position. Then all I have to do is draw the string back. I have done that with the animal actually looking at me, actually raised its head and looked as I completed my draw.

Since my hand is coming straight back, there's not much noticeable movement, and what there is is slow and methodical. That generally is non-alarming. I think the key to it is, since the weapon is so light, I can hold it in the ready position a long time, then draw and release. With a heavier mass weight bow, my bow arm would give out. The best way to avoid that is to wait until the last instant to raise the bow and draw and release, but that necessitates a lot more movement.

SCOUTING A NEW AREA

Walk the boundaries. Walk all the way around the property you're going to hunt, making notes of the trails and the direction the tracks are going on those trails. Then when you find an abundance of tracks heading in a particular direction, go find what those deer are looking for. You'll find either their food source or bedding area.

LOST BLOOD TRAIL

Particularly if it's night and you have a strong flashlight, get down at deer level, scan your light and find the path of least resistance. Even if there's no blood, once you see that tunnel-like path of least resistance, walk out there. I've found half a dozen deer using that technique.

BROADHEAD DESIGN

Howard Hill's belief was that a broadhead should be three times as long as it is wide. I see no reason to argue. I also like a head which cuts all the way from the point to the back tip of the blade; it doesn't lose any energy punching in. I shoot a Simmons Interceptor, which has concave cutting surfaces, which I also like. That concave surface almost looks like it has an ear . If you shoot an animal at a sever angle away from you, that ear seems to rotate around bone and catch there and turn the broadhead into the body cavity of the animal.

The moose I shot in Newfoundland got it that way.

This design also tends to go away from bone. If you hit that "ear" and it catches on the fur and turns the blade tip in, and at the same time it hits a rib, the ear slides around the rib and turns the arrow into the animal.

If you dead-center the rib, the head will split the rib and go on into the vitals.

I have shot animals at severe facing-away angles with an Interceptor and had the arrow head go into the body cavity at a much greater angle than it approached the deer. The arrow actually turned at the rib and went into the deer at an angle that was much more broadside. A head with a straight edge will slide right along the ribs and never go into the vitals.

Sharpening this blade is not difficult. I use a file and a diamond whetstone to finish it. I can put an edge on there that will cut hairs. The edge won't be as smooth as glass....you can feel the tiniest roughness. It's not the rough edge that Mr. Hill liked. I do not want any little bits of meat on the edge of the blade; that reduces penetration and effective cutting. I'm talking a much sharper, smoother edge than the old feather edge people used to talk about.

FIVE PRIORITIES OF BOWHUNTING

#1) Remember what the name of the sport is -- bowhunting. Not bow shooting. A lot of people would have us believe that the most important thing you can do to become a good bowhunter is to learn to drive tacks at 30 yards or 50 yards or whatever. That skill, however, won't do you a bit of good if you're not a good enough hunter to get that animal within good shooting range.

Become a good enough hunter and good enough woodsman to get that animal within your effective shooting range, whatever that range may be, and know what are high percentage shots and what are not.

Some of the most successful bowhunters I know are not that good on the target range. They're good enough, but nowhere near

● *Knowing EXACTLY where to aim is more important than many bowhunters realize. Not every area of the rib cage is a vital area, especially when the animal offers only a quartering shot.*

great. They don't have to be. They're excellent hunters. They get the animal within their distance. Their shots are at unalarmed, relatively relaxed animals.

I remember reading somewhere that the Woodland Indians in the eastern half of the country took shots at whitetail deer averaging three steps. I don't know who did the research, but the point is well taken. They were great hunters....survival hunters.

#2) Know where to aim. Mainly, know a lot more than the broadside shot. I'm continually amazed at the number of bowhunters who aren't sure where to aim if the animal isn't standing broadside. Lack of study is part of the cause. Printed targets with marked kill zones -- all seemingly on broadside views -- also are part of the cause. When a 3-D target is turned at an angle, the kill zone is marked only on the surface, which gives a highly misleading view of things.

Just visualize that basketball in the vital area, as noted earlier in this book, and you'll do fine. You're aiming to the inside of the animal, not the outside.

#3) Know when to shoot. Beyond the basic guidelines, this is not something Byron Ferguson or anyone else can tell you specifically. There is no pat answer, because it is a "read" situation. This knowledge comes from experience. Most of that experience will be gained by hunting and shooting at game, but you also can pick up valuable tips simply by watching animals in the off-season. Or go to a zoo and watch the animals there, see how they move, envision aiming spots and the "when to shoot" instances.

Bowhunting

The basics:

* If the animal's head is behind a tree, come to full draw.
* If the animal's head is down, feeding, come to full draw. But that doesn't work 100 percent of the time.

It's all a matter of having the experience, the knowledge and the feeling of when the time is right to make the shot.

#4) Be accurate enough to hit the aiming spot. Practice. Know your equipment. Again, a lot of this is experience, because there's a tremendous difference between shooting in the back yard in the middle of summer in short sleeves and then sitting up in the tree for four hours in freezing weather, when the shot presents itself and you get only one. You have to make it count. Your muscles are cold. Your heart is thumping. You're shaking from cold and excitement. Under these conditions, being able to hit the aiming spot comes from practical field experience and being able to control your adrenaline rush. The technical skills learned in the back yard are just the jump-off point.

Use the adrenaline rush to focus. You control it, don't let it control you. Put that strength to positive use.

#5) Be a good enough tracker, with the skill and the patience to find the wounded animal. This is especially valuable when you don't do as well as intended with #4. It is not an easy job. Female hunters are the best at it, because they're more patient, which makes them more careful and thorough. Men give up too quickly, cover too much ground trying to find something, and in the process often wipe out whatever sign may exist. I'm not joking when I say this.

The basics:

1) Don't always look at your feet for the sign of where the animal went. Look out in front of you at least 10-15 feet. A lot of times you can see where the animal ran through the leaves, even without a blood trail. Remember to get down at the game animal's eye level and look at things. You might spot a tunnel through the foliage that is unseen from human eye elevation. That's the path of least resistance mentioned earlier.

2) Night tracking -- put some reflector material (aluminum food wrapping material from the kitchen works well) inside the back half of the glass globe. This makes it much easier to see. Night tracking is useful because the phosphorus in blood reflects light well.

3) Be patient. Be careful. Go slow. Be thorough. And remember that a cupful of blood scattered along a trail looks like a lot more than it is. Scatter that same cupful of blood along a trail on snow and it will look like one heck of a lot more than it really is.

● *This is the only way to move a dead moose. Nothing else even comes close, especially when the moose falls roughly eight swampy miles from camp.*

OPERATION MOOSE LIFT

In 1992, I learned a new meaning of the word "pond", learned that some bogs actually have bottoms, and saw my moose airlifted out whole by helicopter. This was in Newfoundland in late October after the rut was completed. It was an educational hunt.

After an uneventful first day, Horace Lane, owner of River Run Outfitters, suggested we try his tent camp located deeper in the wilderness. We arrived in camp early enough for some scouting. After walking about three miles Horace spotted seven moose feeding across a "pond". (If you can't shoot an arrow across it, I would call it a lake.) We noted their location on our topo map and returned to camp to plan.

Next morning Dickey Betts and his guide went out early to find the "Moosezilla" they had spotted while scouting. Horace and I

● *Upper left, when evidence of browsing is a good foot over your head, you fully realize that you're dealing with an extremely large animal, and you think "Oh my...." or something like that. Upper right, the moose where it fell at the edge of a bog and the "greenwood", dry non-swamp mixed spruce and pine. Right, Dickey Betts of the Allman Brothers band plays a couple of songs for Burt Delaney, audio supervisor of the "Land and Sea" television program.*

waited until daylight before paddling a canoe across the five-mile wide "pond". After securing the canoe, we slowly made our way to the bog.

Almost immediately, Horace spotted three cows feeding on the far end of the bog. As we watched the cows, a bull stepped out of the green wood, which in Alabama means "godawful thicket". Our best chance of getting a shot was to stay put and hope the animals would feed toward us.

We had only been there a couple of minutes when a fourth cow with a calf walked up to my right, stopping to look me over. Horace whispered "Get ready, he's coming", so I shifted to a shooting position. The cow saw that and appeared to have several heart attacks before hitting the bog in a full run. Evidently, the bull thought she was running from him. As he crossed in front of me, I swung "Sweet Thang", my favorite hunting bow, into action. When the broadhead touched my finger it was gone. my arrow cut through a rib and angled forward another 20 inches into the chest, going through the liver and taking out the left lung. The rib my arrow sliced off was bigger than an average deer leg, probably 1-1/2 inches wide and nearly one inch thick. The moose went barely 50 yards.

Horace's response (he was directly behind me, standing on tree roots, watching over my shoulder and head), was "Well, you hit it". I thought that was sort of dry. So we gave the moose a few minutes, then went to track. I went to the blood trail, Horace went to look for moose. He found the moose before I found the blood trail. For someone who was so dry, he went goofy. Lots of whoops and hollers. This was the first bow kill he had ever seen.

I found out later the province was concerned moose couldn't be killed with bow and arrow. Far too many previous ones had been hit in the shoulder and lost. The province was considering closing bowhunting for moose. That explained Horace's excitement and relief when the bull went down quickly.

Thoughts on the bow and arrow the first time I got within sight of a moose? I had plenty of confidence. My bow was 75 pounds draw weight; the 2219 arrows were left 31 inches long to get additional weight and tuned for that setup. The arrows definitely were moose arrows. It was after the rut, so they weren't aggressive.

The following year, when Dickey and I went back, I called in a paddlehorn bull. This was during the rut. There was no intention of shooting him; I wanted to play with him. I made a challenge grunt, then raked my bow against a dead spruce tree. Here he came, and he was not happy about this strange new bull in the area. He was redeye angry. He got to 35-40 steps from me and began beating the bark from several trees. I'm sitting there by myself with a bow and arrow, looking at a 1,000 pound upset bull moose, with my guide down at the lake waiting for me. Yeah, I did get a little apprehensive that time. A larger tree would have been nice then.

The main thing in bow and arrow moose hunting -- extremely important -- is that you've got to put your arrow behind the shoulder. They are so big, so massive, you cannot penetrate the shoulder. If you're to take a broadside shot, wait for that near leg to be forward, or take a slightly quartering away shot.

Operation Moose Lift was just that. The helicopters were for the Newfoundland Land & Sea television program use, to carry cameras and other photography gear to appropriate sites. It just happened that they were working with Horace that week. That moose I shot probably is one of the few moose ever transported whole over eight miles of bog and trees.

One other thing. Coming across those bogs at night was a challenge, walking in water on rocks. Newfoundland bogs have nice rock bottoms instead of the mud I expected. However, there are spaces between some of those rocks. When your foot hits one of those spaces, you go all the way up to your straddle in very cold Newfoundland water. This wipes the sleep from your eyes.

THE POWER OF A BEAR

I had been watching the bait one week. It had been hit every night early in the week, but the small logs covering it had only been pushed aside and there were no big bear tracks in the nearby swamp. On Wednesday, things changed. The bait was demolished and those small logs scattered from here to breakfast. We were baiting with pastries, white bread with molasses, and peanut butter and jelly in five-gallon buckets. The bear absolutely loved peanut butter and jelly.

A quick check of the swamp yielded large tracks, 5-1/4-inch front pads. Hoo boy! We rebaited, but this time covered the bucket with a water-soaked log 16 inches in diameter and four feet long. It was so heavy, two of us had to lift it onto the bucket to fasten it in place at the back of the V crib of sticks.

Next morning, the log was 15 yards from bait. We could see where it had been flipped up and made indentations in the ground as it tumbled end over end. The power of a bear is shocking. It's easy to understand why many people are scared silly of bears. They have my full respect and admiration. Signs of their strength, such as that tumbled log that two of us could barely lift, are awe inspiring. This had to be a good- sized bear.

That night, nothing until 15 minutes before quitting time. Then I heard something walking, sounding like a human coming down the ridge, in brush so thick I couldn't see into and not very far to my right. Then the sound stopped. I was ready but nervous. I waited five minutes .... seemed like an hour ... and looked to my left. There stood the bear. It had gone into the bog and its softer, quieter walking, then come in from below.

He sniffed around, walked to the trail that led past my tree stand, got to my stand, put his nose against the tree and then looked up the tree at me. Didn't do anything for my confidence level. If a bear's ears look tiny compared to the size of its head, that's supposed to be a big bear. I was so impressed by its overall size I don't even remember the ears.

The bear turned and walked back to the bait site but showed me only its rear end. No shot. It did a 180, stared up the trail, looked up at me, laid down on its belly about three feet to the side of the bait and rested its chin on its front feet, looking back up the trail I had come in on. It was facing me, looking past me and stayed in that position for what seemed forever.

It was getting darker by the second.

Then he stood up and slowly turned and started to walk away. The trail made a U turn at the bait, went out through the bog to left.

No shot once he got past the curve. But I had a scent rag on a stump about six feet high, with beaver renderings on the scent rag. That caught his attention. He reared up with both feet on the stump, to smell the scent rag. When he did that, I drew the bow. He was broadside. The instant I was ready to release, he dropped down to all fours. That caused me considerable difficulty, because I was already prepared for the shot. I let the bow back down to about half draw and I guess I was getting a little bit of bear fever about this time because I was afraid I wouldn't get a shot. The bow came back up and the arrow was gone.

I thought I heard the arrow hit but was too dark to see for sure. The bear didn't act like a shot bear. It kind of side-stepped, stood for a few seconds looking around, then slowly walked out the trail. I hung my bow on a limb and cupped my hands to my ears to help listen. Stayed that way 10 minutes, because I couldn't hear the death moan. I did hear two low growls but nothing which could be associated with a death moan.

I finally worked up enough nerve to come down the tree, turned my little penlight on, and walked out to where the bear had been standing. My arrow was sticking in a birch limb about the size of your wrist, so I pulled arrow and went back up to trail to meet Fred Pape. Later, we pieced together that the time the bear laid down and was watching up the trail was about the time Fred had driven in. When he turned engine off, the bear stood up and started to leave, but stopped to sniff the scent rag.

We looked at the arrow in the truck's headlights. There wasn't much blood on the arrow. It didn't look good.

Fred had taken his bear that afternoon, so we gathered it up and went back to camp.

Next morning, Jerry Simmons and I went back to track my bear. At the site where I had found the arrow, five feet away was a good blood trail....maroon colored blood, good indication of a liver hit. We found the bear about 35 yards from there.

It expired shortly after my arrow hit it. I was relieved and quite happy. The bear green scored 18-9/16, not a world-beater but an awfully nice bear.

That bear had been fully aware I was in the tree, but it couldn't have cared less. It was conditioned to baiting and probably thought the truck meant someone was coming to bait the site. The hit was a low liver hit. No bones were involved. The bear mostly likely thought it had been bitten by an insect; it surely wasn't alarmed.

• *Ferguson's log-tossing bear, the happy hunter himself, and Santa Claus in a camo suit telling Ferguson that Christmas arrived early this year. Photo by Gary Logsdon.*

TEN MAJOR BOWHUNTING MISTAKES

1. Using wrong approach route to stand.

The most direct route is not always best.

2. Placing stand too high.

The higher the stand, the tougher the shot. There are more obstructions and tougher angles, less chance of double-lung hits. Rule of thumb -- climb in cover or climb high, but only as high as conditions dictate.

3. Mis-reading sign.

To avoid hunting a "cold" stand, learn to age the sign deer leave behind. Many times I have found areas loaded with old sign, but the deer had either depleted the food or simply moved to a more favored food. Make sure the sign you see is fresh.

4. Shooting too soon.

If you shoot the first deer you see, many times you won't see the big one that was just behind it.

5. Trying to force a shot.

Because you may be able to place your arrow accurately is no excuse to attempt a low-percentage shot. Remember that a deer can and will get out of the way of your arrow. Wait for a high percentage angle, i.e., broadside or quartering away, if at all possible.

6. Scouting at the wrong time.

Learn when the deer are the least active and scout then. Since I don't like to hunt in the rain, I will use this time to scout. Most scouting should be done before the hunt.

7. Scouting without a plan.

Scouting is NOT walking around in woods looking for deer tracks. My favorite tactic is to look for food sources, being careful to stay clear of bedding areas. Once a hot spot has been located, I use a compass to note different stand sites for various wind directions.

8. Routine hunting.

Deer will pattern YOU! Break up your routine. Have many more than one or two stand sites ready, so none are overworked and smelled-up and all remain fresh. Stay on stand longer, sleep in, arrive at your stand when you would normally be leaving.

9. Over-hunting.

As hard as it may be, don't hunt the same stand over and over because it seems to be "hot". I have seen many good stands turn cold because of over-hunting. There is too much human scent, too much activity.

There's another form of over-hunting, too. This is the burn-out type you may encounter if you hunt day after day early in the season when your enthusiasm is high. I've seen bowhunters run out of gas, so to speak, before the best hunting -- the rut -- begins. They have lost enthusiasm, or used up all their vacation time, or been gone from home so much that they've had to re-establish cordial relations with their family.

10. Broadheads not sharp.

I mean sharp even after you have hunted a couple of days without shooting them. Check those edges constantly. Weathering and accidental contact with brush can wear them. Just because they're covered by a quiver hood doesn't guarantee continued sharpness.

● *Deer movement is governed by their belly most of the year. When you scout, start with food sources and work from there. Just be sure you're aware of seasonal foods and food sources, and how quickly the deer will move from one to another.*

● Hunting is more than hunting... much more. It varies in all ways and conditions, from spoil-you-rotten outfitted lodges to aches-and pains picnic bench non-camps. But above all ....the land. There's always the land. Hills to climb, hollows to walk, trails to scout....mountain views to drink in and savor....and the next hunt to plan for....tomorrow....next season....forever, we hope.

Bowhunting

Chapter 6
MOST-COMMON QUESTIONS

Q. What is the difference between a Flemish splice string and a continuous loop string?

A. A continuous loop string is a bowstring made from one piece of thread, wound over and over and over on two mounting pegs. The end loops and arrow nocking area are served and the string is waxed.

A Flemish splice string is several pieces of similar length string constructed in such a manner that the loop ends are spliced together in an inter-weaving pattern. The harder you pull, the tighter the splice gets. You can sit on a treestand, waiting for a deer to come by, and actually make a Flemish string. No jig is needed. All you need be certain of is that the strings are the same length, but with ends staggered so as to taper nicely into the body of the string while still forming an adequate loop.

I prefer the Flemish splice string because it is quieter. Usually, I don't even need string silencers unless I want them for tuning purposes. The Flemish string gives off a short, dull, low pitched *thump* when released, whereas the continuous loop string emits a higher pitched, noisier *twang*.

A Flemish string will stretch more when it is new, compared to a continuous loop string of the same length. Allow for that in selecting the right string length.

Q. How do you keep the finger stalls on your shooting glove from taking a permanent crease?

A. You need something strong but reasonably flexible, but which has a memory so it will resume its original shape.

Mr. Hill used a thin strip of whale bone inserted into each finger stall to keep it from taking a groove.

I've been experimenting with different materials. The best thing I've come up with is called "compression rubber". Compression rubber is used in the tool-and-die trade. It is available in rods, from which you can slice pieces. Best size for my glove is one inch length, 1/4-inch width, 1/16-inch thickness. I put a rubber strip into each finger stall, positioned so there's half an inch above and below the bowstring contact point. The rubber is flexible enough that I can bend my end finger joints easily, it's comfortable and it won't shift. It's sensitive enough that I have all the string feel and control I need, yet it's strong enough that it instead of my fingers take most of the weight of the draw.

When you're shooting a heavy draw weight with your fingers, you have to protect them every way you can. The last thing you want is to have your fingers end up looking like spoons...dished and wide at the tips. The best type of shooting glove I've found is made of horsehide. It's thicker than cowhide. This leather is lined with a standard, soft shooting glove leather. Thus, the finger stalls are two layers of leather with an insert between.

My armguard is a piece of heavy latigo leather that I tighten with leather laces.

It's just plain common sense to wear an armguard, no matter which equipment you're shooting. A stung forearm can ruin your concentration. In cold weather when you want to wear a jacket, you need an arm guard to hold your sleeve down so it doesn't interfere with the bow string.

Q. How do you keep fletching from striking and cutting your fingers?

A. I use left wing feathers applied with a left helical twist. They clear my fingers. Right wing feathers, due to the spacing of the leading edge of the fletches, with my hand so close to the shelf, the second hen feather cuts my finger. But with the left wing, it's positioned more in the groove between the shelf and window.

As far as accuracy is concerned, there's no difference between right wing or left wing feathers. However, since the left wing feathers and left spiral give me the necessary clearance, I'm a more accurate shot. I'm not worried about cutting my fingers, so I can concentrate

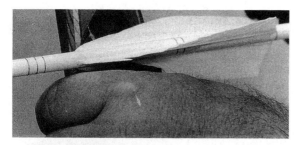

● *Ferguson uses left wing feathers with left helical twist, shown above, for best finger clearance. Right wing feathers with right helical twist turn the second hen feather into his top finger. This is painful and unnecessary.*

on the shot. I can get conditioned to anticipate pain just as easily as anyone else, and I don't like it any more than anyone else.

Q. What is your preferred broadhead?
A. The Simmons Interceptor two-blade, weighing 190 grains. That weight is just the broadhead; it does not include insert weight. I shoot a 75-pound draw weight with 2219 shafts cut to 29-1/4 inches.

Q. What are your thoughts on broadhead alignment?
A. I've shot them with the blades aligned horizontally and with the blades aligned vertically. I can't tell any difference in performance, and as far as trying to align them so they will slip *between* ribs (vertical entry) instead of nicking them (horizontal entry) .... if there was some way I could govern the distance of each shot, so I'd know whether the blades were vertical or horizontal at that specific distance, then I'd be concerned about it. Until then.....

However, there is an advantage to aligning the broadhead vertically and having the shaft cut to the proper length. Once this is accomplished, you will be able to draw to anchor and then, with only a slight stretch, touch your bow hand's forefinger with the back of the broadhead blade. You know you're at full draw, and you have a check to know you remain there. Actually, you cut your arrow so, at full draw, the back of the broadhead almost, but not quite, touches your bowhand forefinger. As you continue that last tiny stretch for full draw, the broadhead touches your finger. It acts like a clicker; you know you're pulling through the shot.

Q. What arrows do you shoot?

A. Aluminum. I don't shoot wood arrows any more. They're too inconsistent, shaft to shaft, in spine, mass weight and performance.

I had the opportunity a few years ago to go to Alaska on a hunt. I ordered 300 dowels for shafts. From that 300, I got exactly a dozen and a half which were suitable for big game hunting. It was just too much work to spine test all of them, weigh them, group them in different lots, and all that. The 18 best shafts I carried with me varied by 20 grains of mass weight and 10 pounds of spine. That is unacceptable.

The old wood is used up. Now we've got green wood that is kiln dried. What happens a lot of times with that wood is that the grain in the shaft actually twists, so it will have a differing spine from back to middle to tip.

Also, if you travel to hunt and should lose or damage your wooden arrows (usually done by the Great Arrow-Stomping Mule), you would be in deep trouble, whereas aluminum arrows are easily replaceable. When you go down to your local pro shop and buy a dozen good grade aluminum arrows, they will be consistent in mass weight and spine...and they will be in stock.

Q. What fletching do you prefer?

A. I prefer a high profile feather, particularly for hunting deer in Alabama or hunting anything anywhere the brush is so thick you have, at best, narrow shooting windows to get your arrow through. I want my arrow to be flying clean as soon as it can; so it will zip cleanly through those narrow shooting windows. Higher profile fletching straightens out that arrow fastest.

● *A high profile fletch stabilizes the arrow fastest. This is critical when you're trying to get that arrow through a narrow shooting opening.*

I won't cut a shooting lane unless I have no other choice. The movement necessary to clear a shooting lane leaves human scent all over the place and physically changes the animal's environment. A trophy buck will definitely notice that change.

I've been shooting the 5-3/4 inch banana cut style which tapers from the middle toward both ends. With this fletch, my arrows are flying clean at about eight paces from the bow, allowing them to fly unhindered through small shooting openings.

I tried a six-inch version of this style but it was noisy. I don't know why. The 5-3/4-inch version I'm shooting now is quiet. I don't know why the noise differential. They worked equally well.

Q. Can vanes be used in place of feathers?
A. No. Vanes are too stiff to shoot off a shelf. They bounce when they hit the shelf and cause the arrows to fly erratically.

Q. How often do you shoot? How many arrows do you shoot a day?
A. Since I work in my shop right behind my house, I am fortunate in that I can practice a couple of times a day, usually about 30 minutes around lunch time and then after work for as long as I want to shoot. That's usually 30 minutes to an hour and a half.

The key is not the amount of time you practice and certainly not the volume of arrows you shoot, but the quality of the time and the quality of each shot. If you can shoot only three arrows a day, if you can put your full concentration on each of those arrows, that will do much more for you than shooting a huge numbers of arrows.

I shoot only three arrows at a time per end, then I pull them. That's the most I can concentrate on super-heavily at a time without a mental rest.

How do you know when enough is enough on any given day? When you become so tired that even with maximum concentration, the arrows still hit erratically in the target.

Q. How do you most easily recognize the line between proper draw weight and over-bowing?
A. Over-bowing is a potential problem with any type of bow, but possibly more so with recurves and longbows. Proper draw weight is whatever you can handle accurately and smoothly and for considerably more than one shot.

The dangers of over-bowing are two-fold. If you're over-bowed, you:

1) won't be able to shoot that bow very well;
2) won't enjoy it, because it's too much work and it physically hurts to shoot the bow.

Shoot a bow that is comfortable and easy to draw. Remember, if you're a bowhunter, there will be times you will sit still several hours in freezing weather ... and then suddenly have to make one shot. There won't be any warm-up shots; the first shot has to count. If that bow strains your milk when you're out in the backyard practicing, imagine what it's going to be like when your muscles are cold, stiff and weakened. This is why it is smart to shoot a bow that is within your means of drawing and shooting well under ALL conditions.

If you're shooting a heavy draw weight compound and want to switch to a longbow or recurve, expect to drop at least 10 pounds in draw weight, maybe as much as 15 pounds.

The bows with no wheels offer peak resistance at different points of the draw than do those with wheels. You have to be fully aware of that difference and be prepared to retrain your mind and muscles for the new pattern of resistance.

Most states have a minimum of 40 pounds, which is sufficient for most circumstances with deer. I don't agree much with requiring an individual to pull a particular weight, because with modern technology and modern materials and supplies, just having a minimum poundage can be misleading.

Poundage is not even a part of the formula to figure kinetic energy, and kinetic energy is what takes the arrow through the animal. I have personally witnessed bows of today in the 50 pound range which will cast the same arrows faster than 90 pound bows of yesterday. I think a better rule would be to require the bow to cast an arrow of a certain minimum weight a certain minimum distance.

Q. What type quiver do you prefer?
A. A back quiver is fun and looks dramatic. I use a back quiver for backyard practice and for small game hunting because it holds a large supply of arrows and I don't need to worry about broadhead sharpness. Any time you're going to shoot several arrows, especially rapid fire stuff, back quivers are just fine.

Big game hunting is a different story. I prefer the hip quiver for hunting big game, especially under typical whitetail hunting conditions, where you may go for days or weeks at a time without firing a shot at game. The volume of arrows simply isn't needed, and the

● *Ferguson's favorite belt quiver began as a bow quiver. It is mounted to the belt so all fletches are in the middle of Ferguson's back. The tube quiver keeps fletching dry and protected in wet weather.*

broadhead blades need to be well protected at all times. But you still want those arrows at the ready position where they are easy to get to. In addition, you may already have a pack of camping gear on your back.

Yes, it's quicker to make a second or a third shot with a back quiver -- if you have the need or opportunity for a second or third shot. But if you, like most of us, seldom get more than one shot at an animal, the hip quiver is fine.

My favorite hip quiver started out in life as a bow quiver. I mounted it to a belt at such an angle that the fletches would be positioned in the center of my back, out of sight of game. The broadheads are right on my hip, because the quiver rides higher than a more traditional side quiver would. I can reach back, with little motion, grab an arrow safely just behind the broadhead, pull it out and slip it on the bowstring. The quiver holds arrow shafts securely and stationary, meaning it won't allow broadheads to dull or shafts to rattle around in the quiver. This setup is highly practical for hunting in heavy brush. The fletches are close enough to my back, and low enough, that I can move through the brush without hanging them up or exposing them to game.

My "roto quiver", a Simmons Bushmaster, is a tube quiver

with a long enough and wide enough opening cut for easy arrow insertion and removal, but small enough to protect the fletching. I like it for rainy weather, to keep the fletching dry. I also like it during gun season (we can bow hunt during our firearms season) to cover my bright fletches -- they're white so I can see them best, but they could also be mistaken for a whitetail flag. I also like the tube quiver if I'm carrying additional gear. I can carry that gear and tube quiver on my back at the same time, because the tube quiver has adjustable carrying straps. And if I want to carry extra arrows, the tube quiver on my back and the belt quiver on my hip increase the arrow payload.

Q. How do you best minimize finger pinch?
A. For a 28-inch draw, any recurve or longbow 62 inches or longer, tip to tip, would minimize or eliminate finger pinch at full draw. Draw lengths under 28 inches won't have finger pinch. You will not see a significant difference in a 62- to a 68-inch bow. Less than 62 inches, finger pinch will be a major factor. This is based on at least a 28-inch draw.

If you have finger pinch, even a slight pluck of the string will be greatly magnified.

Q. What's a good way to judge distance?
A. Judging the prospective flight path and trajectory of the arrow, as explained in Chapter 2, is the way I work it. This is to be used if your goal is to "become the arrow".

If you don't want to use that method, but would rather be a pure gap shooter, first, don't try to judge distance in terms of yards. Judge the distance in terms of steps....your steps. Very few people have a step length of 36 inches, so why bother with yards because it adds another computation, when you really want to keep it fast, simple and accurate. Whether you estimate in individual step counts, or whether you prefer a progression of, for instance, five steps, 10 steps, 15 steps, etc., is totally your decision. Use whatever works best for YOU.

Another method is to look at the ground and estimate the distance halfway to the target. You're dealing with less distance, and you'll most likely be more accurate for that shorter distance. Then simply double the estimated half-distance.

Q. How do you keep your broadheads sharp in the field?
A. This can be a problem if you're using a bag style back

quiver. Howard Hill poured several handsful of oats into his quiver, enough to cover the broadheads and hold them more or less far enough apart. Carrying a sharpening steel is almost a necessity. When you break for lunch, check the broadheads. If they're not sharp enough to cut a hair on your arm, then you need to sharpen them. There just isn't any shortcut.

The best way is to protect the edges with vaseline or masking tape. Some heads are supplied with a plastic cover. Nothing is perfect. Rust-inhibiting oil may leave an unwanted odor. Vaseline collects dirt and other junk. You can forget to remove the tape or the plastic cover before shooting the arrow.

The most practical all-around method is to check the blades, touching them up or replacing them when necessary.

● A small flat file and a steel, especially diamond-imbedded steel, are excellent in-field sharpening tools. They're light and easily carried. Make it a habit to check your broadheads for sharpness when you break for lunch each day, or at any consistent time.

Q. How far can a longbow be shot accurately? How far can any bow be shot accurately?

A. It's a matter of the operator. Any bow can be made to shoot more accurately than any person could ever shoot it. It's the difference between mechanical and physical.

There IS a practical limit to a bowhunting shot distance. That's what the questioner usually means when asking the "how far...." question. A bow can be shot accurately to whatever your personal limits are, for the reason given in the first paragraph. In actuality, that distance may be farther than conditions allow on any given shot.

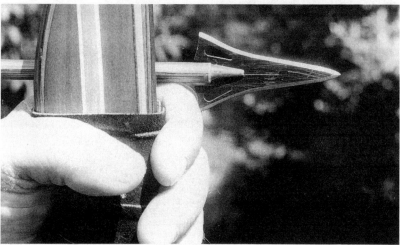

● Cut your arrows so the back of the broadhead blade, mounted vertically, is a fraction of an inch from your bowhand index finger when you reach full draw. Your final stages of maintaining full draw and breath control will pull the broadhead back to touch your finger, acting much like a clicker, and that's when you release.

Chapter 7
Building A Longbow

When designing a longbow, the first thing to be decided is what you want that bow to do. If you want the bow to be extremely fast, or if you want it to be extremely forgiving, or if you want it to be a combination of the two. Then decide how you're going to go about doing that.

There are a limited number of devices available to make the bow shoot faster, and there also are a limited number of devices available to make that bow more stable. So you plan the two together as well as possible with the priorities you set.

When I designed my first bow, I designed it to be as fast as I could make it. All the design features were meant to produce a fast arrow. Then I started taking away some of the speed, to build stability back into it while sacrificing the least amount of speed.

Speed, when you're talking about a traditional longbow, can be accomplished by back set and by limb tip action, how far the tip is moved from the braced position to full draw. Back set is the distance the limb tips are forward of the centerline of the handle when the bow is unstrung.

The first bow I designed had 1-3/4 inches of back set. It was fast, but it also was unstable. So I couldn't have hit anything with it. The faster the bow, the less stable it will be. By the laws of physics, they don't go together.

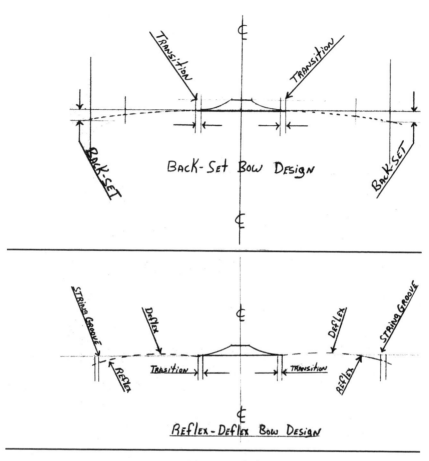

BACK-SET BOW DESIGN

REFLEX-DEFLEX BOW DESIGN

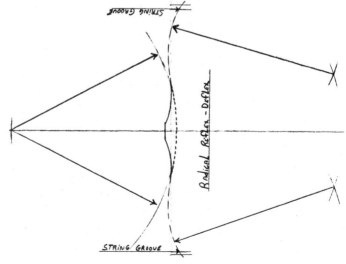

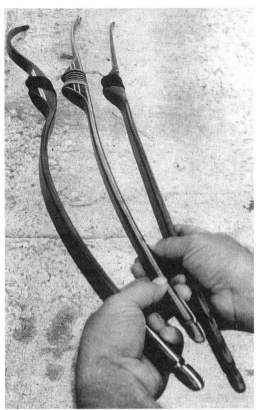

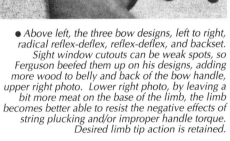

• *Above left, the three bow designs, left to right, radical reflex-deflex, reflex-deflex, and backset. Sight window cutouts can be weak spots, so Ferguson beefed them up on his designs, adding more wood to belly and back of the bow handle, upper right photo. Lower right photo, by leaving a bit more meat on the base of the limb, the limb becomes better able to resist the negative effects of string plucking and/or improper handle torque. Desired limb tip action is retained.*

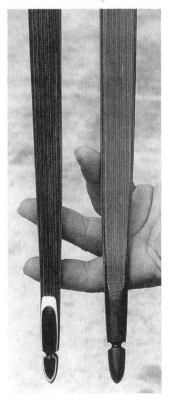

Building A Longbow

I made that bow stable by modifying the back set so it applied only to the outer 13 inches of the limb, nearest the string groove. Those outer 13 inches of limb had 75 percent of the total back set distance. The remaining 25 percent of the back set was applied from there to the base of the limb, the fade-out. This enabled me to leave the base of the limb wider, while at the same time achieving limb tip action on the narrowing tip. I left enough meat on the base of the limb to pull the tip back and make the string track down the center of the limb when I had a bad release.

What makes a bow unstable? If the limb itself is so delicate that upon the release, if you pluck the string or move the bow arm, you can make it do bad things. Let's say you pluck the string. Visualize when you pull the string out of the limb tip groove with the pluck. If you release at that point, the tip oscillates, trying to make the string fire down the center, but there's not enough meat on the base of the limb to make it right itself.

By leaving the base of the limb wider and applying a good percentage of the back set at those outer 13 inches of the limb, I was able to get the same limb tip action as with a narrower limb, the string travel was just as far from the brace position to full draw as with a narrower limb. The meat remaining on the base section of the limb, however, made that limb base -- actually, the entire limb out to that 13-inch mark -- strong enough to resist the effects of plucking the string or torquing the bow handle. That heavier limb base would, in effect, pull the string back into alignment and make it fire down the center of the limb.

I modified the side profile by grinding the limb narrower.

Another way to achieve limb tip action is by using tapered laminations. The laminations taper from the butt end to what will be the limb tip. The farther you go in the string groove area, the thinner the lamination will be. That serves to weaken the limb tip, allowing more limb tip travel, which gives you a longer power stroke and thus stores more energy, while retaining stability in the major part of the limb.

I used parallel laminations (same thickness over entire length) in that first bow I designed. They are more stable, but they're also slower because they add weight to the limb tip. They're less flexible, too, so you will get less limb tip travel.

I felt there still was a better design feasible, so with my second bow I began experimenting with tapers. I moved the base of the back set one inch out onto the limb base to allow that point more flexibility. When I had the back set beginning at the fade-out, the limbs often would snap off like they'd been hit with an axe. There simply was too much stiffness, not enough flexibility, at that point. It was a good shooting bow. I shot 13 deer with a prototype.

Through further experimentation, I've come to believe that a combination of tapers works best. I use what I call a Double 0 2 taper, which is a taper of .002 of an inch in thickness through the length of the lamination. This goes on the back of the limb. I use a Double 0 1, a taper of .001 of an inch, for the belly of the limb (the side facing the shooter). That works best in producing a relatively fast bow with good stability.

Then I began experimenting with multiple laminations, more than just two or three. I built bows with as many as five laminations of action wood, which is a multiple laminate material itself. Five laminations produced a great shooting bow, but the increase in performance didn't seem to be worth the increased expense in materials and man-hours to add that fifth lamination. So we dropped to four laminations, and that's where we have remained on our top-of-the-line bows. We have two parallel and two tapered laminations in those bows. The two parallels are in the center, sandwiched between the tapered laminations.

Our top-line bows also have reflex deflex limbs rather than the straight back set. Reflex deflex simply means that the limb crosses the profile center line of the bow twice. The deflex part is closest to the handle and is the part which angles toward the shooter. That makes the bow more stable, with less hand shock upon release. The reflex part is the outer section of the limb and angles away from the shooter. It is the same as back set and imparts speed to the bow.

These bows have proven superior in performance. They're fast and stable, so they're highly shootable.

I went so far as to design a longbow that is a radical reflex deflex. A recurve bow is a radically reflexed deflexed bow. Some people who have seen this radical longbow of mine called it a semi-recurve.

What I wanted to do with this particular design was to create a bow that would shoot at least as fast as the recurve bow, but yet build into it the performance characteristics of longbow. That principally being the forgivingness or stability of the longbow. This effort worked well; the Patriot in our line is designed this way and is extremely fast. To enhance the speed, it is built to accept a Fast-Flight string. A 50-pound Patriot with a 28-inch, 2213 aluminum arrow will shoot through a chronograph at more than 190 feet per second.

The latest bow I designed has five laminations, but the fifth lamination is made of bias glass. We do this in our Royal Safari bow. It has a slight reflex deflex, with two parallel laminations of action wood, two tapered laminations of action wood, and the bias glass lamination through the core of the bow. The bias glass through the

• The grip is shaped so the bow hand pushes in toward the centerline at a 15 degree angle. This forces the bow to torque consistently, so the potential negative effects are neutralized.

• String grooves are cut so the shoulders are level so the string loop will remain in the groove instead of sliding out and twisting the limb. The string groove also is cut with side relief to hold the loop more securely and keep the loop from slipping down the limb.

• To guarantee proper arrow clearance and minimize drag, the shelf and window are crowned. Crowning also helps negate torquing effects.

core makes the bow smoother to shoot, tougher and extremely stable. The bias glass resists twisting of any kind. In addition, there's not as much hand shock, and it increased the bow's speed by about five feet per second.

I shape the grip so the bow hand pushes in toward the centerline (vertical axis) of the handle, at a 15 degree angle from the center of the original grip. This ensures that the bow hand is to the left of the center line of the bow (for a right hand shooter). This forces the bow to torque, which is what I want it to do, and it forces the bow to torque the same every time. That consistency is what is needed. I have designed that feature into the handle, because in shooting a longbow, we have no way to counter the torque.

The torque is taken care of in the drawing of the bow, before the string is ever released. This makes the torque an integral part of the unit ... I have allowed for it ... and therefore the potential negative effects of torque are neutralized.

The handles in our top-of-the-line bows are designed a bit differently in the cutout area for the sight window. The sight window obviously is the weakest part of the bow. To strengthen that area, I add more material than has traditionally been used, so the sight window is deeper, has more wood, from back to belly of bow. It's like extending the handle farther up, running it into the limb base, and then cutting the sight window out of that. The shelf can be cut to the same depth, but there's more meat front to back for retained strength.

Then we added uni-directional bow glass through the profile center of the handle. It reinforces the sight window, keeping it from twisting. The uni-directional glass will bend forward and back, if needed, but it will not bend side to side.

To guarantee proper arrow clearance and minimize drag, the shelf and window are crowned. Longbows don't have to have crowned sight windows, but they shoot much better when they do. Remember, too, that crowning helps negate torquing effects. To negate torquing effects even further, I grind a 30 degree relief into the front of the sight window on the far side of the center line.

String grooves used to be a sore point, because cutting them was inexact. The shoulders of the string grooves should be level. If one shoulder is lower than the other, it will allow the limb to twist because the string will be more likely to slide out of the groove. The string groove also must have relief -- cut into each side of the limb -- to hold each side of the loop more securely, keep the loop from slipping down the limb tip and twisting the limb. This relief also extends string life because it doesn't wear as much on the strands. The recent addition of a machine I designed has helped considerably in cutting the string grooves with exactness.

The handle doesn't need to be wrapped, but I prefer it. I like a wrap over a solid piece, because it gives me reference points for hand and finger position. Regular suede leather works just fine. A solid wrap becomes slick with use, which certainly adds a challenge to holding onto it.

In bowstring material -- Fast-Flite and Dacron -- I prefer Fast-Flite. It is much more durable. Regarding speed, a Fast-Flite string with silencers attached is about the same speed as a Dacron string without silencers. Fast-Flite also has less stretch and doesn't need to be retuned as often. It is a bit noisier, but string silencers will take care of that problem.

Serving material that will hold securely on Dacron will slide on Fast-Flite. The best I've found for Fast-Flite strings is a #2 nylon. Monofilament is more difficult to work with and wears out gloves and tabs faster. It also comes loose easier, and once it is loose there's no fixing it.

The Dacron string is a great string; don't get me wrong on that point. It is larger diameter for equal strength, so once you get accustomed to shooting Fast-Flite, then switch to Dacron, the Dacron feels like a rope on your fingers. That bulkiness means slower speed and more hand shock upon release. Dacron is a more forgiving string material and will cause less grooving in the glove.

A knowledgeable bowyer should be able to measure the individual archer, talk to him briefly about his shooting style, his form, any problems he may be having shooting, whether he's currently shooting a longbow, what his goals are, and measure his physical dimensions....then be able to design a bow -- the length, the tapers, the way the limbs are ground, the handle shape for torque control -- for the individual that he can shoot well. He should be able to shoot that bow better than any bow he ever had, because that's what a custom bow should be.

A custom bow is much more than putting your name on it, much more than having a bow cut to a particular draw length.

The method I use for determining the length of the bow to best fit the archer is to measure his draw length AND the length of his arms, because draw length and length of arms are not always that closely related. The variants on draw length include the degree of openness of his stance, whether he leans at the waist, where he anchors, etc. As a benchmark to measure his draw, I use a 68-inch bow. Reason for this is that an archer with a 28-inch draw, shooting a 68-inch bow, will be bending that bow and loading those limbs all the way to the handle, assuming he's using the standard 14-inch handle and riser section, without overstressing.

For every inch or fraction of an inch his draw varies from the 28-inch benchmark, I double that and deduct that total from the length of the bow. For instance, if an individual has a 27-inch draw, that's one inch difference from 28. Doubling that makes two inches, which are deducted from a 68-inch benchmark. This archer will best shoot a 66-inch bow.

If someone is concerned only with hunting, I'll recommend a bow shorter than normal. For instance, I'll recommend a 64-inch bow instead of a 66-incher. We all tend to short-draw the bow in a stress situation. Through testing I have learned that a bow made to exactly fit a particular draw -- if that bow is short-drawn by one-half inch, it will lose as much as 12 feet per second in arrow speed. The same style and same draw weight bow, but slightly shorter, short-drawn the same one-half inch, will lose only four to six feet per second.

I'll leave the handle length the same unless we get into the really short bows....less than 60 inches.

Chapter 8
Children's Hospital Benefit

Alabama Archers
Annually Raise Money For Needy Young Patients
by John Sloan

Each Spring, a group of bowhunters and other archers gather in Alabama for a weekend of fun and entertainment. It's all to benefit a worthy cause. The first Children's Hospital Invitational Tournament, in 1992, drew more than 200 traditional archers from four states.

Hosted by the Alabama Society of Traditional Bowmen, the event raised nearly $5,000 for the Alabama Children's Hospital. Open only to archers with traditional equipment, this tournament features more than simply shooting arrows at 36 targets and some flying discs.

It is a fun gathering. There is a lot of trading, buying and selling of products by the participants. Lots of camaraderie and a night of special entertainment are included. The entertainment featured Dickey Betts, lead guitarist and song writer with the Allman Brothers band, Gary Morris, country music superstar, and Shaun Ferguson and the Straight Shot Band.

The event started when Byron Ferguson, internationally known bowyer and traditional archer, was asked to host a tournament with proceeds to go to a charity of his choosing. The first tournament was held at Stillwaters Plantation near Dadeville, Alabama. Some $2,500 was raised for the Children's Hospital in Birmingham.

● Ferguson presents a check for nearly $5,000 to Kay Emack, coordinator of special projects for Children's Hospital.

In 1992, the site was changed to the Shelby County Bowhunters range in Columbiana, Alabama. Ferguson, realizing he could not personally attend to all the details of the tournament, enlisted the aid of the Alabama Society of Traditional Bowmen. Under the leadership of president Pat Carter, with the help of Corky Briggs and Sylvester Shaw, things began to take shape and guidelines were developed.

"This is a fun tournament," said Carter. "We are not pushing competition or winning the tournament. This is just about having fun and helping the children's hospital. We have a barbecue dinner, special entertainment, campfires and blanket trading. This is an annual event for the entire family. You can have a ball here even if you don't shoot a bow.

"We aren't looking for a permanent home for the tournament. We want to move the location each year and make this the premiere archery event in Alabama. This year, the range belongs to the Shelby County Bowhunters.

"Actually, we are growing so quickly, we need a larger area. Eventually, we will find a permanent location that fits all our needs," predicts the society's president.

"In one year, we have undergone a tremendous change," said host Byron Ferguson, "Last year, the money raised for the hospital

● *Ferguson and Dickey Betts are interviewed by local television, top photo. Below, Ferguson coaches Taylor Perkins as she begins learning the "become the arrow" system of shooting.*

came from donations. This year, all the money raised from entry fees, the dinner, the show, the novelty shoots and everything else is going to the hospital. I expect we will reach or exceed $5,000 this year. And it will get bigger."

The tournament is open to traditional archery only — longbows and recurves — but any arrow may be used. There are classes for men, women and youths with separate recurve and longbow classes in each. There are also some novelty shoots, including John Freeland's SXT disc launcher. It is not only a novelty shoot, but is a required part of the competition

Ferguson, with the mechanics of the tournament in the capable hands of the ASTB, turned his attention to securing some special guests. His first calls went to close friends Dickey Betts and Gary Morris. Betts, author of the crossover hit by the Allman Brothers, "Ramblin' Man," and famed lead guitar virtuoso, is a 30-year veteran of bowhunting.

"When Byron called and told me what he was doing, I was quick to agree to participate," Betts said. "I was at the tournament last year and had a ball. This year is even bigger and more fun. How can you not get involved with a charity like this and have this much fun?"

Gary Morris, best known for his smash hit of "Wind Beneath

My Wings," is another accomplished longbow shooter. "I just go where Byron tells me," he said. "The day before yesterday, I was in Seattle; last night, Atlanta. Tonight, after I leave here, I go to Dallas. I think I am going to enjoy today as the best of them all. Shoot some arrows and raise some money for those kids. Heck of a deal."

With some celebrities in place, Byron Ferguson turned his attention to gathering corporate sponsorship to offset costs. "I figured the more we could get donated or paid for, the more money would go to the kids," he said. Among those corporate sponsors were Easton Aluminum, Marriot Courtyard of Hoover, Alabama, Buckhunters Unlimited and Ferguson Adventure Archery. "But there is no way to remember all of the people who contributed goods, time and energy to this project," declared Ferguson.

Kay Emack, coordinator of special projects for Children's Hospital, gives us an idea of what was involved. "In 1991, our hospital treated 169,000 children," she said. "In the 81-year history of our hospital, our mission has always been to treat all children, regardless of their ability to pay. That is why fund raising endeavors such as this tournament are so important.

"We are located in Birmingham, but we treat children from all counties of the state. What the Alabama Society of Traditional Bowmen and Mr. Ferguson have done is just wonderful. I'm not a bow person yet, but this is such fun and these are such nice people, I may have to learn. This is just tremendous."

Maybe Byron Ferguson explained it best: "Everything that I've ever done as far as my archery is concerned, in the whole scheme of things, doesn't mean anything compared to this. This means a lot. This is conserving our most precious natural resource: the children. If I do nothing else in my life other than this one tournament, at least I have made a contribution by lending my name to the tournament. I am proud of the fact."

The tournament continues to grow and new locations are being explored. For more information on the dates and location of the tournament, contact: Byron Ferguson, P.O. Box 1314, Hartselle, AL 35640.

As the publicity for the tournament says, "Come see our country's best archers in action."

Whether you are a blanket trader, bowyer, arrowsmith, craftsman, fun shooter, competitor or spectator, there will be fun and companionship for all to enjoy. Bring your chairs, blankets, family and friends. Spend a slow-paced, traditional rendezvous weekend with old and new friends. And help ill or injured children in the bargain.

The Publisher

Glenn Helgeland is president of Target Communications Corporation (TCC). He has published 12 archery/hunting/wild game cooking books under his TCC banner and has several more scheduled.

Helgeland is the producer of five deer/turkey hunting shows:
*Wisconsin Deer & Turkey Expo, Madison;
*Michigan Deer & Turkey Spectacular, Lansing;
*Illinois Deer & Turkey Classic, Bloomington;
*Ohio Deer & Turkey Expo, Columbus;
*Tennessee Deer & Turkey Expo, Nashville.

He has been involved in archery and bowhunting 30 years. He edited *Archery World,* now *Bowhunting World,* magazine 11 years, 1970-1980, and won awards from the National Archery Association for service to archery and from the National Shooting Sports Foundation for a series of articles titled "The Hunter's Story".

He has been at various times bowhunting columnist for *American Hunter, North American Hunter* and *Bowhunting World.*

Helgeland co-authored with John Williams, 1972 Olympic archery gold medalist, the book "Archery For Beginners". He also edited the 2nd edition of the Pope and Young Club's Big Game Records Book.

He was named, in 1985, as one of the "50 Who Made A Difference" to the sport of archery/bowhunting over the previous 15 years, by the publishers of *Archery Business* magazine.

Before becoming involved in archery/bowhunting writing and publishing, Helgeland was an associate editor of *National Wildlife* magazine.

The "On Target" Series of Outdoor Books
from Target Communications Corporation (TCC)

UNDERSTANDING WINNING ARCHERY, Hall of Fame Commemorative Edition, by Al Henderson, coach of the 1976 U.S. Olympic Archery Team. Mental control means better shooting results, easier archery gear set-up and tuning, more-productive practices, and winning archery – target, field and hunting.
122 pages. ISBN: 0-913305-00-6. $12.95

TAKING TROPHY WHITETAILS, by Bob Fratzke w/ Glenn Helgeland. In-depth, detailed information on year-round scouting and its huge payoff, scrape hunting, rut hunting, late season hunting, camo, use of scents, mock scraping and licking branches. *140 pages. ISBN: 0-913305-02-2. $10.95*

TO HECK WITH GRAVY wild game cookbook, by Glenn & Judy Helgeland. Great meals from quick, easy recipes; don't be tied to the kitchen. Includes 209 recipes – roasts, steaks, marinades, soups/stews, ground meat, fish, birds. Plus field dressing, meat handling/processing tips, spice chart, low-sodium diet tips.
120 pages. ISBN: 0-913305-05-7. $12.95

TASTY JERKY RECIPES, by Glenn & Judy Helgeland. Spicy, mild, sweet and no-sodium recipes for three meat cut thicknesses and tenderness; gives you three different tastes for each recipe.
$2.00 plus stamped, self-addressed #10 return envelope

TUNING YOUR COMPOUND BOW (4th Ed), by Larry Wise. Two new chapters -- Hybrid cams, and 3-D tuning & shooting for bowhunting. All cam info updated. High performance tuning for all cams, all compounds. Chapters on round wheel, single cam & super-cam setup and tuning, making/serving/repairing strings & cables, pre-use bow preparation, draw stroke, power stroke, shooting from the valley, fine-tuning, test shooting, tuning FastFlite cable system, building & tuning aluminum and carbon arrows.
152 pages. ISBN: 0-913305-19-7. $13.95

TUNING & SILENCING YOUR BOWHUNTING SHOOTING SYSTEM (3rd Ed), by Larry Wise. Problem-solving info on fitting bow (compound, recurve, longbow) to your body style & shooting form; broadhead effects on arrow flight; noise reduction throughout entire system; aiming/shooting strategies; proper practice; plus much of the compound setup and tuning info in Tuning Your Compound Bow.
170 pages. ISBN: 0-913305-08-1. $13.95

BECOME THE ARROW (the Art of Modern Barebow Shooting), by famed archery trick shot Byron Ferguson w/ Glenn Helgeland. Details the "become the arrow" philosophy; explains how to visualize arrow flight path and sight picture; shooting form practice and mental exercises; tuning for barebow shooting, bowhunting details and more. *BOOK - 112 pages. ISBN: 0-913305-09-X. $13.95*
VIDEO (VHS - 45 min.). UPC 8-29493-12467-9. $19.95
DVD. UPC 8-29493-12467-6. $19.95

THE WILD PANTRY wild game cookbook, by Glenn & Judy Helgeland. 200+ recipes (steaks, roasts, goulash, stews, Mexican, jerky, sausages [patties, links, summer, etc.]; mostly venison, but upland birds, fish, waterfowl. You'll enjoy the stories and anecdotes about wonderful (and some not-so-wonderful) wild game cooking experiences and meals; we've all been there. *156 pages. ISBN: 0-913305-13-8. $12.95*

CORE ARCHERY, by Larry Wise. Learn proper back tension and much more. This is a systematic set of shooting form steps built around the proper use of your skeleton. Throughout each form step, the governing theme is to maximize skeleton and minimize muscles, for optimum results. If you do this, your form will be energy efficient, fatigue resistant and highly repeatable. *144 pages. ISBN: 0-913305-18-9. $13.95*

To Order:
1) See your local sporting goods dealer
2) Go to our web-site -- *www.deerinfo.com*
3) Call 1-800-324-3337 (M-F, 8:30 am - 4:30 pm CDT)

- **All prices (books & s/h) are in U.S. funds**
- **WI residents add 5.6% tax.**
- **MC/VISA accepted**
- **Shipping/Handling**
  $3.00/order (book rate)
  $3.50/order (1st Class)

Write or call for a FREE information flyer and order form:
TARGET COMMUNICATIONS CORPORATION
7626 W. Donges Bay Rd., Mequon, WI 53097
262-242-3990 • 1-800-324-3337 • mac@deerinfo.com • www/deerinfo.com